Japanese Flower Arrangement
ENCHANTING
IKEBANA

DISTRIBUTORS:
UNITED STATES: Kodansha America, Inc., through Farrar, Straus & Giroux, 19 Union Square West, New York, NY 10003.
CANADA: Fitzhenry & Whiteside Ltd., 195 Allstate Parkway, Markham, Ontario L3R 4T8.
BRITISH ISLES AND EUROPEAN CONTINENT: Premier Book Marketing Ltd., Clarendon House, 52, Cornmarket Street, Oxford, OX1 3HJ England.
AUSTRALIA AND NEW ZEALAND: Bookwise International, 54 Crittenden Road, Findon, South Australia 5023.
JAPAN: Japan Publications Trading Co., Ltd., 1-2-1, Sarugaku-cho, Chiyoda-ku, Tokyo, 101-0064 Japan.

First edition 1996, 3rd printing July 2000
Original Copyright © 1996 by Reiko Takenaka
World rights reserved by JOIE, INC. 1-8-3, Hirakawa-cho, Chiyoda-ku, Tokyo 102-0093 Japan;
Printed in Hong Kong.

ISBN0-87040-984-0

ACKNOWLEDGMENTS

My grateful appreciation to the following individuals for their encouragement and patience throughout the many months it took to compile this book.

Shiro Shimura, publisher, JOIE, INC.
Yoshiki Nakano, photographer
Yoko Ishiguro, translator
Akira Naito, chief-editor
Mitsue Hashimoto, Mieko Baba, editors

Reiko Takenaka

FOREWORD

Ikebana is hospitality from the heart, using various plants and flowers. It is an art in which the force of life expressed in living plants and the spirit of the person arranging them speak deeply to each other and unite to create new beauty and form. By devoting one's heart to flowers, one can in an informal, natural way provide pleasure for family and guests. Ikebana brings a richness to our lives!

I have been trying to modify the traditional forms of ikebana to adapt to today's lifestyle. "Japanese Flower Arrangement: IKEBANA", my first book, published in 1995, was more favorably received than I had expected; perhaps my easy and practical concepts met the readers' needs. I am very happy that they would like a new edition.

I produced this book to acquaint as many people as possible with the joy and delight of ikebana. I have avoided strict rules of traditional arrangement in order to allow myself total freedom in creating ikebana which is suitable to the space it occupies. For vases I have used common household articles, showing how new beauty can be created with originality when using only a few flowers. Here indeed is the charm of ikebana.

I have explained how to arrange flowers so that anyone with a little skill and sensitivity can do ikebana. I will be happy if this book brings you pleasure.

What makes ikebana rewarding is the heightened sensitivity of those who do it. Giving thanks for the bounties of nature, I hope to continue my activities to make ikebana into a living and creative art form.

Flowers convey a heartwarming message which crosses the barriers of nationality and language. I would like to express my heartfelt thanks to the JOIE, INC., publishers of this book, for their assistance and friendship.

Reiko Takenaka

June 1996
Tokyo

CONTENTS

LIVING ROOMS

Elaborate arrangements aren't proper for rooms where the family gathers. Just a few flowers anchored in an everyday container create a warm, relaxing atmosphere.

1 **A medley of colors and shapes are harmonized in the clear lines of the bulrush.**
Materials: Bulrush, Lace flower, Larkspur, Gerbera
Containers etc.: 3 rectangular *suiban* (shallow contaianer), 3 *kenzan* (needlepoint holder)
Finished size: H60 cm × W110 cm × D32 cm (23½" × 43" × 12½")
See page 84 for arranging steps.

2

Simply modern: The curvy line of allium leek is balanced with a short upright stem and a rose.

Materials: Rose, Allium leek
Container: Miniature vase
Finished size: H 25 cm × W 36 cm × D 23 cm
(10″ × 14″ × 9″)

● **Arranging Steps:**

Hold allium leek, its cut end touching the inner wall of the vase. Slant right, resting the stem on the rim of the vase. Rest the rose on the other side of the vase. Stand a short stem of allium leek upright to finish.

3

Delicately spreading yellow-leaf spirea create an image of spring with fresh foliage.

Materials: Camellia, Yellow-leaf spirea
Containers etc.: Basket with lid, Small vessel, *Kenzan* (needlepoint holder)
Finished size: H 45 cm × W 60 cm × D 45 cm
(17½″ × 23½″ × 17½″)
See page 86 for arranging steps.

LIVING ROOMS

4   The richness and heaviness of grapes are lightened with a single sheer pink curcuma, the focal point of the arrangement.

Materials: Grape, Curcuma alismatifolia
Container: Glass vase
Finished size: H 58 cm × W 58 cm × D 36 cm (22½″ × 22½″ × 14″)
See page 84 for arranging steps.

Arrange branches bearing fruit so they appear as natural as if they were growing in the garden.

5 The natural contour of mild spray mums create a rich spaciousness with fragrant fruit as the focal point.

Materials: Chinese quince, Spray mum
Container: Tube-shaped vase
Finished size: H 82 cm × W 72 cm × D 51 cm (32″ × 28″ × 20″)
See page 85 for arranging steps.

LIVING ROOMS

6 Understated humor. An unexpected combination of yellow balls and globe thristle behind fan-shaped iris leaves.
Materials: Yellow ball, Iris leaf, Globe thristle
Containers etc.: Empty can, *Kenzan* (needlepoint holder)
Finished size: H57 cm × W49 cm × D31 cm (22¼″ × 19″ × 12″)
See page 88 for arranging steps.

Informal arrangements done imaginatively in tins.

7

Carefully choose floral materials to go with the hues and the patterns of the container you are going to use. Here, a lone lily complements an antique-looking can.

Finished size: H 36 cm × W 60 cm × D 16 cm
(14″ × 23½″ × 6½″)

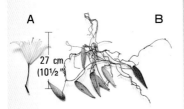

Materials:
A: Oriental hybrid lily
B: Kapok

Container:
H 27 cm × W 10 cm × D 5 cm
(10½″ × 4″ × 2″)

● **Arranging Steps:**

1

Position the lid to give a slightly askew look. Let kapok vine cascade down both sides.

2

Finish with a lily, slanting it a little left.

8

Scotch broom can create a delicate and luscious effect, however roughly it is arranged. Lobster claw provides the focal point.

Materials: Scotch broom, Lobster claw
Containers etc.: Empty tin, *Kenzan* (needlepoint holder)
Finished size: H 50 cm × W 68 cm × D 49 cm (19½″ × 26½″ × 19″)
See page 87 for arranging steps.

ENTRANCES

Greet your guests with a welcoming, cheerful arrangement of your own. Show what you can do with flowers of the season.

9 A harmony of straight and curvy lines. Eye-catching anthuriums are positioned to make you feel welcome.
Materials: Spirea (pink), Monstera, Anthurium
Container: Irregular-shaped vase
Finished size: H 55 cm × W 64 cm × D 46 cm (21½″ × 25″ × 18″)
See page 86 for arranging steps.

10

An airiness is achieved by combining clear water, the gentle movement of branches and the soft hues of flowers.
Materials: Yellow-leaf spirea, Dendrobium orchid, Baby's breath, Lily, Marguerite, Gerbera, Ageratum, Cantabury-bells
Container: Glass vase
Finished size: H 40 cm × W 90 cm × D 35 cm
(15½″ × 35″ × 13½″)
See page 91 for arranging steps.

Make a free and easy arrangement to show the best of natural lines.

11 The flowing lines of iris leaves contrast with the lovely budding branches in this composition, welcoming spring.
Finished size: H 45 cm × W 73 cm × D 45 cm (17½" × 28½" × 17½")

● Arranging Steps:

54 cm
(21")

Materials:
A: Iris leaf
B: Tulip
C: Corylosis Pausiflora

A   B   C

Container:
Water jug
H 20 cm × Diam 9 cm
(8" × 3½")

Right-side view of finished arrangement

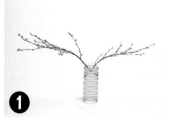

1 Place 2 long branches, slanting low toward both sides, cut edges touching inside walls of vase.

2 Add more twigs to give fullness.

3 Center tulips so they slant forward.

4 Add iris leaves to back and front of tulips creating a streamlined effect.

ENTRANCES

12

Free-forming colored wire twined about the sober oak creates a mobile for the eye. For impact use red only.

Finished size: H 63 cm × W 40 cm × D 28 cm (24½″ × 15½″ × 11″)

58 cm
(22½″)

A   B

Materials:
A: Withered oak
B: Hibiscus
Free-forming colored wire

Container:

Irregular-shaped vase
H 16 cm × W 35 cm
(6½″ × 13½″)

● **Arranging Steps:**

❶

Stretch free-forming wire and twine around withered branch.

❷

Secure the branch in the right opening.

❸

Finish with hibiscus facing upwards.

Enjoy juxtaposition of combining dry and fresh materials.

13

The flimsiness of curvy willow is enhanced with tissue paper. The paper works as a foggy background for the hydrangea.

Materials: Hydrangea, Willow (salix matsudana tortuosa), Wrapping tissue, Paper glue
Container: Glass vase
Finished size: H 41 cm × W 51 cm × D 28 cm
          (16″ × 20″ × 11″)
See page 88 for arranging steps.

14

Delicately crossed summer cypress softens the color and shape of the lobster claw.

Materials: Lobster claw, Colored summer cypress
Container: Tube-shaped vase
Finished size: H 78 cm × W 90 cm × D 34 cm
          (30½″ × 35″ × 13″)
See page 89 for arranging steps.

ENTRANCES
15

Flat factor of the leaf is modified into expressive lines and form with a little technique.

Finished size: H45 cm×W50 cm×D45 cm (17½″×19½″×17½″)

61 cm
(23¾″)

A

B

Materials:
A: Barroom plant
B: Dahlia

Container:
Irregular-shaped vase
H22 cm×Diam 7.5 cm
(8½″×3″)

● **Arranging Steps:**

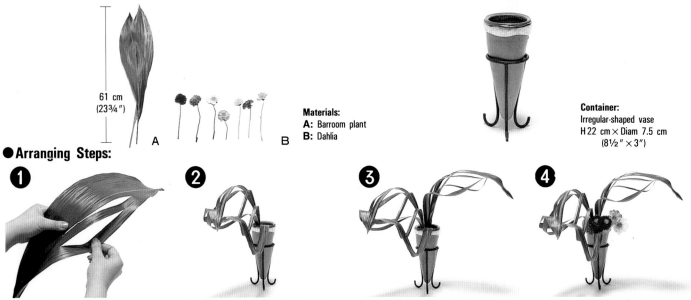

❶ Tear the middle section of barroom plant leaf.

❷ Place in vase slanting left so the torn side hangs down.

❸ Add the other leaf to back right.

❹ Fill the rim of vase with dahlia facing forward.

For entrances, combine cheerful and inviting blossoms to give everyone a lift.

16 The base of the arrangement is not covered so the lively movement of tulips can be emphasized.
Materials: Cherry blossom, Tulip
Containers etc.: Narrow rectangular vase, *Kenzan* (needlepoint holder)
Finished size: H 68 cm × W 68 cm × D 41 cm (26½″ × 26½″ × 16″)
See page 89 for arranging steps.

JAPANESE ROOMS

Decorate the alcove to match the serenity and solemnity of Japanese room. Remember to position the arrangement at eye level when seated on the floor mat.

17 Uncomplicated arrangement using few materials for a calm and relaxing air.

Materials: White enchianthus, Peony, Thunbergii
Container: Irregular-shaped vase
Finished size: H49 cm × W64 cm × D54 cm (19″ × 25″ × 21″)
See page 92 for arranging steps.

Show the best of natural stem lines for a nonchalant mood.

18 Arrange leafy arrowwood branches to their best advantage. Flowers are used so as not to disturb the line.

Finished size: H 70 cm × W 60 cm × D 60 cm (27¼″ × 23½″ × 23½″)

● **Arranging Steps:**

Center arrowwood slanting slightly towards your left shoulder. Show the best side of the branch.

Place shorter branch at center, slanting low towards front right.

Fill in base with spray mum facing forward.

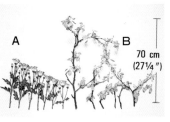

Materials:
A: Spray mum
B: Arrowwood

Container: *Suiban* (shallow contaianer)

H 10 cm × W 27 cm × 18 cm
(4″ × 10½″ × 7″)
Place *kenzan* (needlepoint holder)

19

A miniature rose branch has many different aspects. Select the best angles for each branch.

Materials: Miniature rose, Privet
Container: Tube-shaped vase
Finished size: H 55 cm × W 72 cm × D 49 cm
(21½″ × 28″ × 19″)
See page 92 for arranging steps.

JAPANESE ROOMS

 Simple but charming accent in subdued surroundings.
Materials: Hydrangea
Container: Tube-shaped vase
Finished size: H 45 cm × W 49 cm × D 32 cm (17½″ × 19″ × 12½″)
See page 93 for arranging steps.

76 cm
(29½")

A

Materials: Kerria

21

Expressive kerria blossoms seem to dance on these flowing branches.

Finished size: H 27 cm × W 80 cm × D 64 cm (10½" × 31¼" × 25½")

Container:
Irregular-shaped vase
H 27 cm × W 16 cm × Diam 5 cm
(10½" × 6½" × 2")

● Arranging Steps:

❶ Place kerria **A** in the right mouth of container slanting left.

❷ Place additional curvy branch to give volume and to conceal the rim of vase.

❸ Add several shorter branches slanting right.

❹ Cover the rim of left mouth with blooming branches, slanting low.

WINDOWSILLS

A windowsill is a perfect place to shed light on your arrangement. Window displays should look good both from inside and outside.

A
72 cm
(28")
B

Materials:
A: Smokebush
B: Gerbera

Container:
Glass jar
H 20 cm, Opening diam 2 cm
(8", ¾")

●**Arranging Steps:**

1 Stand smokebush upright in the center.

2 Set gerbera within the leafy area of smokebush. Be sure to draw together all stems.

  A center of color enhances the sunlit, lacy smokebush.
Finished size: H 71 cm × W 71 cm × D 50 cm (27½" × 27½" × 19½")

● **Arranging Steps:**

①

Set sea holly in the container so the flowers are secured in container.

②

In the center, stand vanda orchid in an uprising form.

③

Fill in with oncidium orchid by adding behind.

23

Show your skill in a dramatic display like this.

Finished size: H 37 cm × W 31 cm × D 22 cm
(14½" × 12" × 8½")

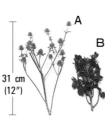

A   B   C

31 cm
(12")

Materials:
A: Sea holly
B: Vanda orchid
C: Oncidium orchid

Container:
Wine glass
H 20 cm × Diam 7 cm
(8" × 2¾")

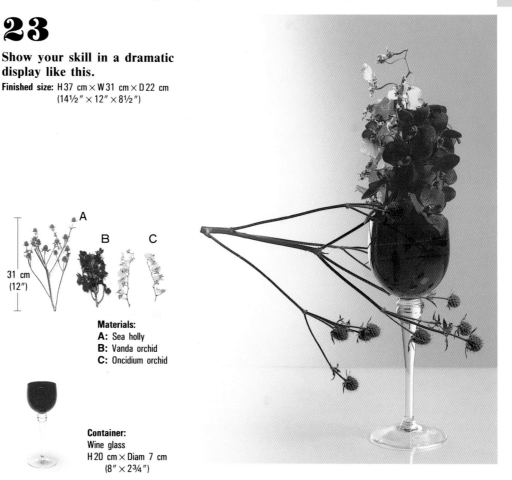

24

Pointed Astilbe flowers give this soft and warm pastel arrangement depth and dimension.

Materials: Gerbera, Astilbe
Container: Miniature tin bucket
Finished size: H 37 cm × W 45 cm × D 34 cm
(14½" × 17½" × 13")

See page 93 for arranging steps.

25

The bamboo-like leaves of the golden-rayed lily and cattail signal a light and breezy effect.

Materials: Bamboo-leaf lily, Cattail
Container: Glass vase
Finished size: H 63 cm × W 58 cm × D 35 cm
(24½″ × 22½″ × 13½″)

See page 94 for arranging steps.

26

The cool beauty of foliage tumbling from a frosty-looking glass vase.

Materials: Stomona japonica, Smokegrass
Container: Glass vase
Finished size: H 54 cm × W 72 cm × D 50 cm
(21″ × 28″ × 19½″)

See page 94 for arranging steps.

Warm sunlight gives your flowers prominence and full expression.

27

Detached straight lines make a strong contrast with the soft circular flower and the distinctive Monstera leaf.

Materials: Allium giganteum, Wisteria, Monstera
Containers etc.: Empty can, *Kenzan* (needlepoint holder)
Finished size: H 72 cm × W 64 cm × D 64 cm
(28″ × 25″ × 25″)

See page 95 for arranging steps.

28

A welcome arangement of the familiar sunflowers and lilies, softened with the green of smilax vine.

Materials: Sunflower, Glory lily, Smilax
Container: Irregular-shaped vase
Finished size: H 64 cm × W 60 cm × D 35 cm
(25″ × 23½″ × 13½″)

See page 90 for arranging steps.

TABLE ARRANGEMENTS

For restful times of the day, decorate your table with an uncomplicated display of flowers. Strong-scented materials should be avoided for dining tables.

29   **A light and feathery arrangement with the horizontal lines of fern and the delicacy of Scabiosa.**
Materials: Scabiosa japonica, Miniature rose, Baby's breath, Leather fern
Container: Irregular-shaped vase
Finished size: H 45 cm × W 76 cm × D 37 cm (17½″ × 29½″ × 14½″)
See page 90 for arranging steps.

Overflowing flowers create a lively, modern look.

30 **A wooden container complements this casual and cheerful arrangement.**
Materials: Strawberry candle, Baby's breath, Larkspur, Tulip, Yomena aster, Star-of-Bethlehem, Asparagus fern
Containers etc.: Planter, Small vessel, *Kenzan* (needlepoint holder)
Finished size: H 45 cm × W 64 cm × D 40 cm (17½″ × 25″ × 15½″)
See page 96 for arranging steps.

31

Bright amaryllises take visual precedence in this collection. Notice the diagonal line from left to right.
Materials: Amaryllis, Barroom plant, Prairie gentian, Sweet pea, Begonia, Lapeirousia, Larkspur, Lobster claw
Container: Deep oval bowl
Finished size: H 32 cm × W 46 cm × D 35 cm
(12½″ × 18″ × 13½″)
See page 97 for arranging steps.

TABLE ARRANGEMENTS

32   **A cool look is evoked when the airy lines of kangaroo grass waft above water.**

Materials: Hydrangea, Kangaroo grass
Container: Glass plate
Finished size: H 45 cm × W 76 cm × D 36 cm (17½″ × 29½″ × 14″)

● **Arranging Steps:**

Shape hydrangeas into rounds, and float on water. Stand kagaroo grass between hydrangeas.

Be sure a centerpiece is low enough to be viewed well from above.

33

Romance in a wine glass. Beargrass is used to express a refined nonchalance.

Materials: Beargrass, Larkspur, Sweet pea
Container: 1 pair wine glasses
Finished size: H 23 cm × W 58 cm × D 27 cm
(9″ × 22½″ × 10½″)

● **Arranging Steps:**
Fill one glass with larkspur, and the other with sweet pea. Add beargrass to both.

34

Delicate, pastel flowers seem to rock in a boat of leaves.
Finished size: H 20 cm × W 68 cm × D 20 cm (8″ × 26½″ × 8″)

68 cm
(26½″)

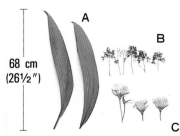

A
B
C

Materials:
A: Curculigo
B: Larkspur
C: Prairie gentian

Container:
Cocktail glass
H 10 cm × Diam 11 cm (4″ × 4½″)

● **Arranging Steps:**

1 Cover the rim of glass with two pairie gentians. Place the longer one slanting low towards left.

2 Frame the center prairie gentians with larkspur in a dome shape.

NOOKS & CRANNIES

You are free to set flowers wherever you like. Choose a well-traveled place and your arrangement will give you pleasure every time you see it.

A scene from an autumn field in a nostalgic vase to enrich the rustic tones.

Materials: Billberry, Cattail, Super lady, African lily
Container: Empty tin
Finished size: H 87 cm × W 60 cm × D 63 cm (34″ × 23½″ × 24½″)
See page 98 for arranging steps.

36

The cheerful colors and form of tulips set in a narrow vase attract attention.

Finished size: H 64 cm × W 64 cm × D 49 cm (25″ × 25″ × 19″)

● **Arranging Steps:**

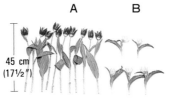

A   B

45 cm
(17½″)

❶

Arrange tulips from the center of container towards your right shoulder.

Materials:
A: Tulip
B: Miniature tulip

❷

Add more tulips to face left, grading levels.

Container: Tube-shaped vase
H 36 cm × Diam 9 cm
(14″ × 3½″)

❸

Fill the vase with miniature tulips.

37

A flamboyant mix of contrasting hues and shapes.

Materials: Oriental hybrid lily, Kangaroo paw, Rose hip, #30 wire

Container: Glass vase

Finished size: H 40 cm × W 49 cm × D 32 cm
(15½″ × 19″ × 12½″)

See page 95 for arranging steps.

NOOKS & CRANNIES

38

Brighten up the room corner with a bold and cheerful display.
Materials: Sunflower, Cucumber-leaf sunflower
Containers etc.: Bucket, *Kenzan* (needlepoint holder)
Finished size: H 50 cm × W 58 cm × D 45 cm (19½″ × 22½″ × 17½″)
See page 100 for arranging steps.

Distinctive shapes create a dramatic focal point in your home.

39

An amusing fox face resting on long serrated leaf could tell a humorous story.

Materials: Fox face, Ficus kookaburra
Container: Miniature pitcher
Finished size: H 13 cm × W 31 cm × D 11 cm
(5″ × 12″ × 4″)

● **Arranging Steps:**
Slant ficus leaf almost horizontally towards left.
Place fox face fruit at the base and on the spout.

40

Unaffected combination of tropical leaves to make everyone relax.

Materials: Alocasia, Monstera, Baby's breath, Verbena tenera
Container: Glass vase
Finished size: H 63 cm × W 86 cm × D 58 cm
(24½″ × 33½″ × 22½″)

See page 100 for arranging steps.

BEDROOMS

Bedrooms are for relaxation. Fresh flowers placed on a shelf, dressing or bedside table will ease your mind after a long and hectic day.

41

The sweet hues of flowers convey a calm and restful mood.

Finished size: H32 cm × W81 cm × D40 cm (12½″ × 31½″ × 15½″)

● Arranging Steps:

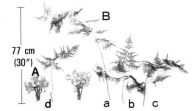

Materials:
A: Peruvian lily
B: Asparagus fern

77 cm
(30″)

Container:
2 cocktail glasses
H16 cm × Diam 5.5 cm (6½″ × 2½″)

①

Brim each glass with Peruvian lily.

②

Insert asparagus fern so they flow over each side.

34

The subtle perfume of flowers will give you pleasant dreams.

● **Arranging Steps:**

Arrange spirea branches so they spread naturally towards both sides.

Slant orchid right. Place sweet peas low, slanting forward.

42 Spring is around the corner; create the feeling with the flowing lines of spirea.

Materials: Spirea, Oncidium orchid, Sweet pea
Containers: 2 glass vases

Finished size: H 45 cm × W 76 cm × D 53 cm
(17½″ × 29½″ × 20½″)

43 Creeping vine creates a special space between the table surface and flowers.

Materials: Kujaku aster, Prairie gentian, Red vine
Containers etc.: Irregular-shaped vase, *Kenzan* (needlepoint holder)
Finished size: H 32 cm × W 71 cm × D 50 cm
(12½″ × 27½″ × 19½″)

See page 102 for arranging steps.

BEDROOMS 44

Dainty larkspur in a vertical design, for a soft and gentle air.
Materials: Larkspur, Wormwood
Containers etc.: Accessory case, 2 *kenzan* (needlepoint holder)
Finished size: H 58 cm × W 23 cm × D 20 cm (22½″ × 9″ × 8″)
See page 101 for arranging steps.

45

The harmony of colors and the silhouette remind one of a prima donna dancing in the field.

Finished size: H 37 cm × W 19 cm × D 20 cm (14½″ × 7½″ × 8″)

● Arranging Steps:

1

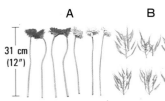

A   B

31 cm (12″)

Bunch 7 gerberas and wire just below flower heads.

Materials:
A: Gerbera
B: Rape seed
30 wire

2

Container:
Irregular-shaped vase
H 13 cm × Diam 13 cm
(5″ × 5″)

Center gerberas and fill the base with rape seed.

3

If gerberas cannot be secured with rape seed, use *kenzan* (needlepoint holder).

46

The rich and heavy texture of lilac is lightened by the feathery petals of prairie gentian.

Materials: Prairie gentian, Lilac
Container: Mug
Finished size: H 37 cm × W 41 cm × D 31 cm
(14½″ × 16″ × 12″)

See page for 101 arranging steps.

KITCHENS

Make a casual arrangement using everyday kitchenware. Your favorite dishes will take on a new personality.

47

Bring the tranquility of a Japanese garden inside with fresh green horsetails and muted flowers.

Materials: Horsetail, Sedum erythrestictum, Yellow ball
Containers etc.: Casserole, *Kenzan* (needlepoint holder)
Finished size: H 58 cm × W 23 cm × D 13 cm (22½″ × 9″ × 5″)
See page 39 for arranging steps.

Make a pop-art display using vegetables from the kitchen.

●Arranging Steps for 47:

Container:

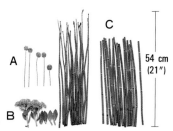

H 4 cm × W 23 cm × D 13 cm (1½″ × 9″ × 5″)
Lay *kenzan* (needlepoint holder)

A
C

B

54 cm
(21″)

Materials:
A: Yellow ball
B: Sedum erythrestictum
C: Horsetail

48

Many vegetables have beautiful shapes. Here shiny, fresh peppers are fixed to the splinters of dried foliage.

Materials: Horsetail, Asparagus fern, Dried briar, Pepper
Container: Tube-shaped vase
Finished size: H 78 cm × W 95 cm × D 68 cm (30½″ × 37″ × 26½″)
See page 103 for arranging steps.

❶

Bunch horsetails in varying heights, and stand upright.

❷

Place sedum low in the front.

❸

Stand yellow ball stems between horsetails and yellow balls, in varying heights.

BATHROOMS

A simple arrangement of flowers in a clear glass will brighten up your bathroom.

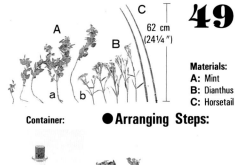

C
62 cm
(24¼")

A

B

a   b

Container:

49

Materials:
A: Mint
B: Dianthus
C: Horsetail

Delicate dianthus flowers and mint create a soft and warm atmosphere as well as giving the room a pleasant aroma.

Finished size: H 68 cm × W 53 cm × D 45 cm (26½" × 20½" × 17½")

●Arranging Steps:

Flat-sided bottle
H 13 cm, Opening diam
1.5 cm (5", ½")

❶ Place mint (a) and (b), crossing each other to cascade down.

❷ Add shorter sprigs of mint to give volume.

❸ Center dianthus inclining a little forward.

❹ Insert horsestails slanting a little left. Bend one stem so the tip points backwards.

40

50 **Contrasting shapes and colors salute each other to bring a suggestion of spring sunshine.**
Materials: Yomena aster, Ear of barley, Flowering fern
Containers: 2 glasses
Finished size: H 41 cm × W 32 cm × D 22 cm (16¾″ × 12½″ × 8½″)
●**Arranging Steps:**
Put yomena aster in left container to form a dome shape. Be sure to cover the rim of container. Fill right container with ears of barley, and stand fern upright in varying heights.

Use clear glass containers for a crisp and cool feeling.

HOW TO ENJOY A FLOWER TWICE:

If you want to enjoy your favorite flowers for a longer time, first arrange them using the full length of the stems, then remove any faded or dead flowers, cut and rearrange them.

SPRAY MUMS

I) USING FULL LENGTH:
Show the best of spray mum in a dome-shaped arrangement.

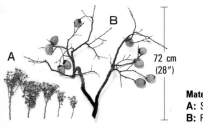

A: Spray mum
B: Persimmon

72 cm
(28")

51 Ripe persimmons with their spindly branches bring the country air of autumn into your home.

Finished size: H 81 cm × W 86 cm × D 40 cm (31" × 33½" × 15½")

Materials:
A: Spray mum
B: Persimmon

42

II) CUTTING SHORT: Create a brand-new image by floating the flowers.

Container:

Glass bowl
H 5 cm × Diam 9 cm
(2″ × 3½″)

Extra small glass
H 5 cm × Diam 5 cm
(2″ × 2″)

Rectangular plate
H 4 cm × W 28 cm × D 28 cm
(1½″ × 11″ × 11″)

52

Floating flowers move continuously recreating the arrangement.
Finished size: H 23 cm × W 41 cm × D 28 cm (9″ × 16″ × 11″)

● Arranging Steps for 52:

18 cm
(7″)

Set small glass in bowl.

Place kapok, resting the head on the rim of container.

Cut off stems.

Be sure to pour in water before floating the blossoms.

Materials: A: Spray mum
B: Kapok

A

B

● Arranging Steps for 51:

Container:
Tube-shaped vase
H 31 cm × Diam 9 cm
(12″ × 3½″)

1 Hold persimmon branch upright.

2 Stand in vase securely.

3 Fill the vase with spray mums facing forward.

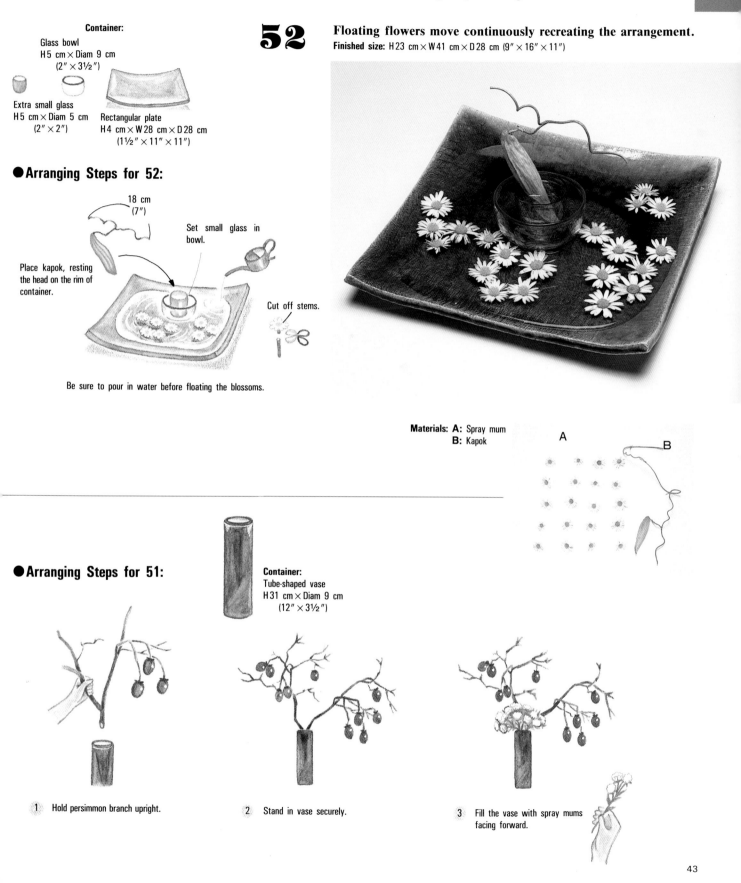

I) USING FULL LENGTH: Vary the lengths to create an illusion of motion.

53 Barroom plant foliage expresses stability with its vertical stance while marguerites give dimension.

Finished size: H 59 cm × W 68 cm × D 45 cm (23″ × 26½″ × 17½″)

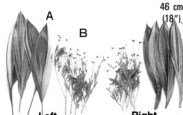

A

B

Left arrangement

Right arrangement

46 cm (18″)

C

Right-side view of finished arrangement.

Materials:
A: Barroom plant
B: Marguerite

C: Washi paper
(to cover milk cartons)
Paper glue

II) CUTTING SHORT:

Choose flowers that are still fresh and use them to decorate the base of an arrangement.

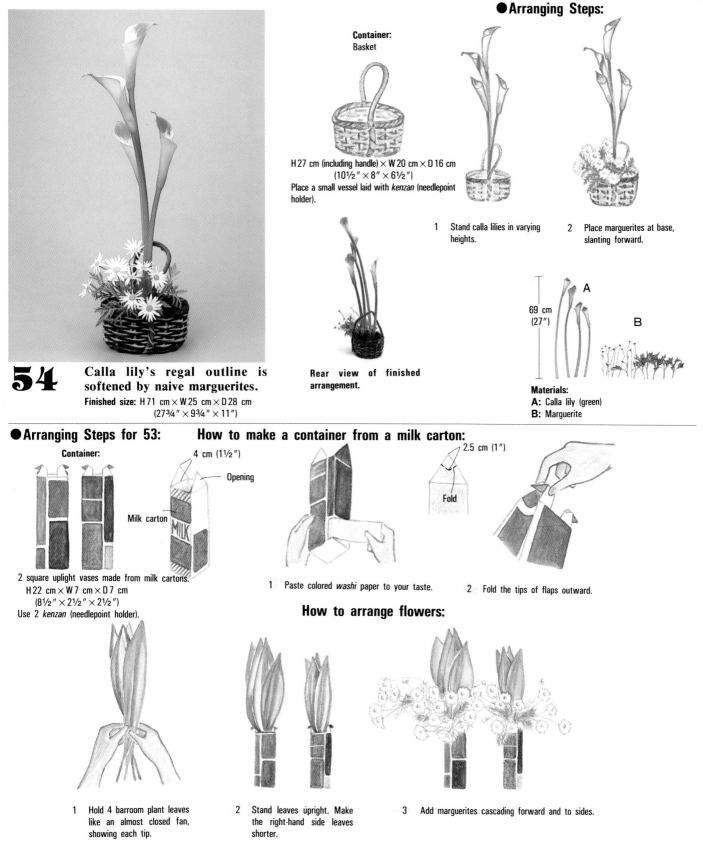

●Arranging Steps:

Container:
Basket

H 27 cm (including handle) × W 20 cm × D 16 cm
(10½″ × 8″ × 6½″)
Place a small vessel laid with *kenzan* (needlepoint holder).

Rear view of finished arrangement.

1   Stand calla lilies in varying heights.

2   Place marguerites at base, slanting forward.

69 cm
(27″)

Materials:
A: Calla lily (green)
B: Marguerite

54

Calla lily's regal outline is softened by naive marguerites.
Finished size: H 71 cm × W 25 cm × D 28 cm
(27¾″ × 9¾″ × 11″)

●Arranging Steps for 53:

Container:

2 square uplight vases made from milk cartons.
H 22 cm × W 7 cm × D 7 cm
(8½″ × 2½″ × 2½″)
Use 2 *kenzan* (needlepoint holder).

How to make a container from a milk carton:

4 cm (1½″)

Opening

Milk carton

MILK

2.5 cm (1″)

Fold

1   Paste colored *washi* paper to your taste.

2   Fold the tips of flaps outward.

How to arrange flowers:

1   Hold 4 barroom plant leaves like an almost closed fan, showing each tip.

2   Stand leaves upright. Make the right-hand side leaves shorter.

3   Add marguerites cascading forward and to sides.

HOW TO ENJOY A FLOWER TWICE: **HYDRANGEAS** (DRIED)

I) **USING FULL LENGTH:** Show the natural lines for an artistic look.

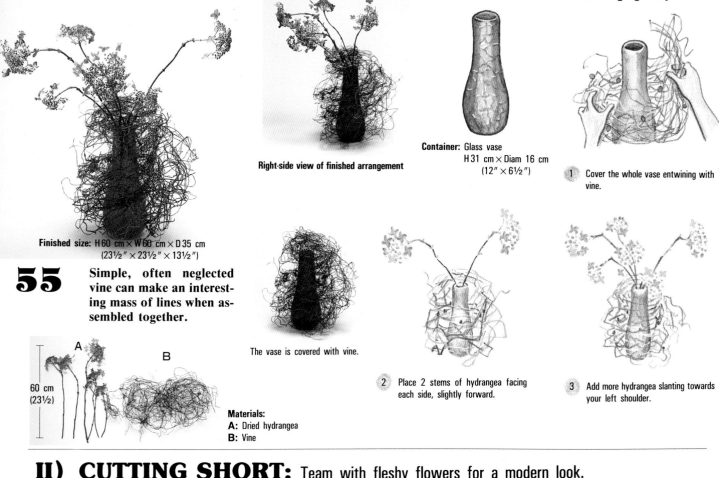

Right-side view of finished arrangement

Container: Glass vase
H 31 cm × Diam 16 cm
(12″ × 6½″)

●**Arranging Steps:**

1. Cover the whole vase entwining with vine.

The vase is covered with vine.

2. Place 2 stems of hydrangea facing each side, slightly forward.

3. Add more hydrangea slanting towards your left shoulder.

Finished size: H 60 cm × W 60 cm × D 35 cm
(23½″ × 23½″ × 13½″)

55

Simple, often neglected vine can make an interesting mass of lines when assembled together.

60 cm
(23½)

A

B

Materials:
A: Dried hydrangea
B: Vine

II) **CUTTING SHORT:** Team with fleshy flowers for a modern look.

●**Arranging Steps:**

Container:

Speckled vase
H 18 cm × W 13 cm × D 7 cm
(7″ × 5″ × 2½″)

1. Place hydrangea facing forward, in varying heights.

Purple heart

2. Add purple heart in center slanting forward.

Materials:
A: Dried hydrangea
B: Purple heart

56

Capture the essence of faded flowers and show the textural contrast with fresh ones.

Finished size: H 32 cm × W 27 cm × D 19 cm
(12½″ × 10½″ × 7½″)

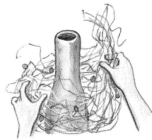

22 cm
(8½″)

A

B

HOW TO ENJOY A FLOWER TWICE: MINIATURE MAPLES/ROSES

I) USING FULL LENGTH: Show the best of the natural curves.

57
Autumn-tinted maple leaves combined with red, leafless branches create depth above miniature roses.

Finished size: H 69 cm × W 81 cm × D 83 cm (27″ × 31½″ × 32½″)

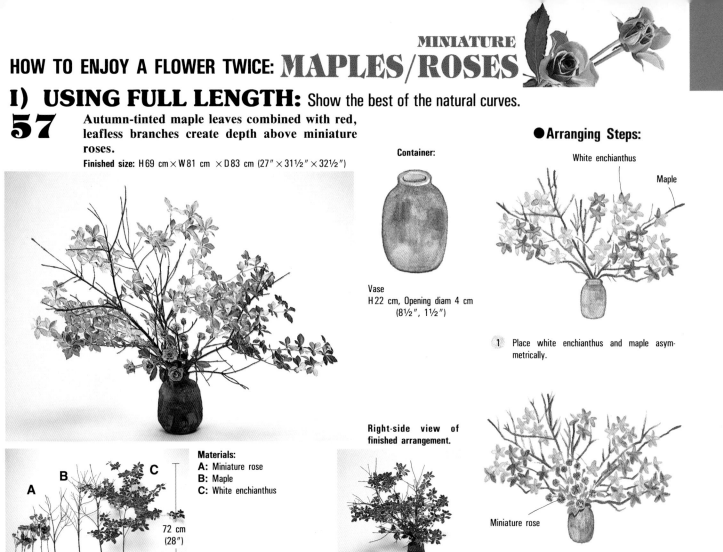

Container:

Vase
H 22 cm, Opening diam 4 cm
(8½″, 1½″)

Right-side view of finished arrangement.

Miniature rose

Materials:
A: Miniature rose
B: Maple
C: White enchianthus

72 cm
(28″)

● **Arranging Steps:**

White enchianthus

Maple

1 Place white enchianthus and maple asymmetrically.

Miniature rose

2 Fill the base with miniature roses slanting forward.

II) CUTTING SHORT: Treasure the last blossoms and twigs.

22 cm
(8½″)

Materials: **A:** Miniature rose
B: Maple
C: Fallen leaves
D: Vine

Container:

Large *sake* cup
H 5.5 cm × Diam 10 cm
(2½″ × 4″)

● **Arranging Steps:**

Stand twig upside down.

Float a single rose.

Make rings with wild vine and link them.

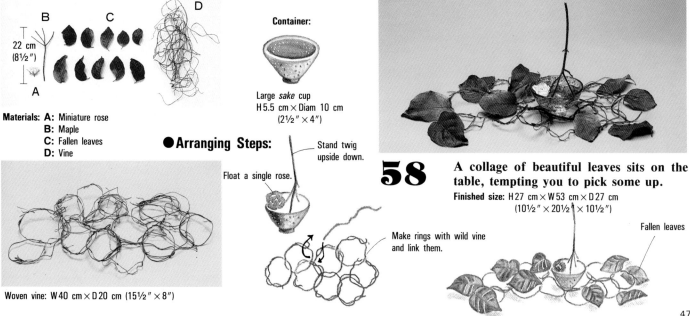

58
A collage of beautiful leaves sits on the table, tempting you to pick some up.

Finished size: H 27 cm × W 53 cm × D 27 cm
(10½″ × 20½″ × 10½″)

Fallen leaves

Woven vine: W 40 cm × D 20 cm (15½″ × 8″)

TWO DESIGNS USING ONE CONTAINER

Flowers can look surprisingly different, depending on the shape and size of the container. In other words, the container evokes unexpected charm. Try to find a good balance between the flowers and the container.

■ LOW, BROAD CONTAINER: Set in lines, carefully.

Container:

H 16 cm × W 23 cm × D 10 cm
(6½″ × 9″ × 4″)

59 A focus on curvy line.

Extend the space to one side showing the best of the vine movement. This arrangement has three factors: line, color, and dimension to express delicacy.

Finished size: H 31 cm × W 50 cm × D 31 cm (12″ × 19½″ × 12″)

Rear view of finished arrangement

Right-side view of finished arrangement

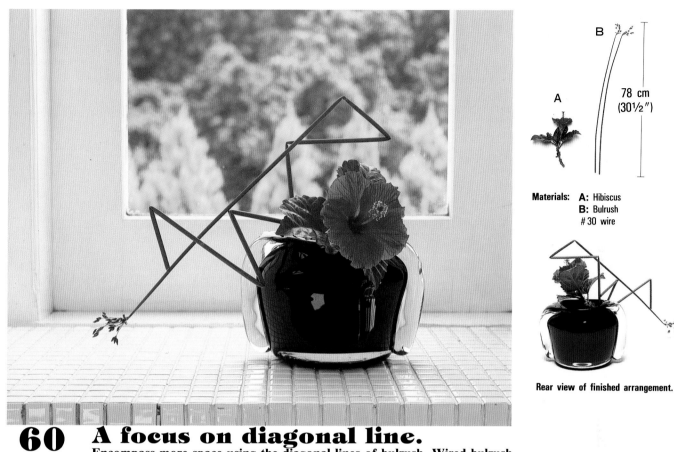

Materials: **A:** Hibiscus
B: Bulrush
#30 wire

78 cm (30½″)

Rear view of finished arrangement.

60 A focus on diagonal line.

Encompass more space using the diagonal lines of bulrush. Wired bulrush can be shaped into any form you like. Here, easy geometric shapes cotrast with the spherical hibiscus.

Finished size: H 34 cm × W 45 cm × D 27 cm (13″ × 17½″ × 10½″)

●**Arranging Steps:**

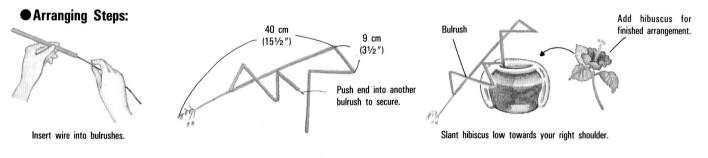

Insert wire into bulrushes.

40 cm (15½″)

9 cm (3½″)

Push end into another bulrush to secure.

Bulrush

Add hibiscus for finished arrangement.

Slant hibiscus low towards your right shoulder.

●**Arranging Steps for 59:**

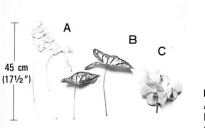

45 cm (17½″)

A

B

C

Materials:
A: Bleached vine
B: Caladium
C: Vanda orchid

Do not layer leaves

1   Set vine almost horizontally. Place orchid.

2   Add caladium for finished arrangement.

TWO DESIGNS USING ONE CONTAINER

■ SMALL, CYLINDRICAL CONTAINER:
Stress either lines or leaves.

Container:
H 18 cm × Diam 9 cm
(7″ × 3½″)

61 A focus on width.
Simple but dramatic contrast of leaf shapes with textured cockscomb, the focal point.
Finished size: H 49 cm × W 49 cm × D 58 cm (19″ × 19″ × 22½″)

Left-side view of finished arrangement.

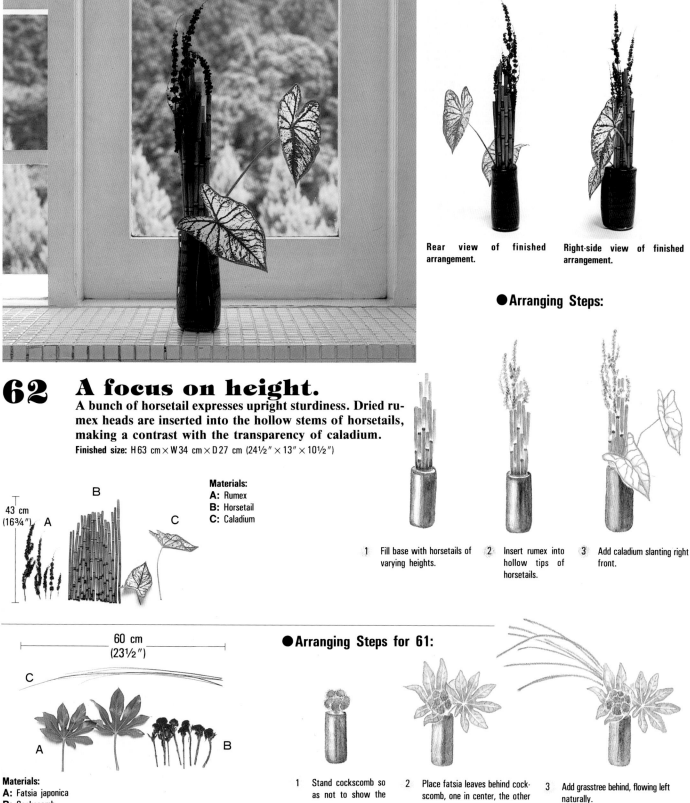

Rear view of finished arrangement.

Right-side view of finished arrangement.

62 A focus on height.

A bunch of horsetail expresses upright sturdiness. Dried rumex heads are inserted into the hollow stems of horsetails, making a contrast with the transparency of caladium.

Finished size: H 63 cm × W 34 cm × D 27 cm (24½″ × 13″ × 10½″)

43 cm (16¾″)

A

B

C

Materials:
A: Rumex
B: Horsetail
C: Caladium

●Arranging Steps:

1 Fill base with horsetails of varying heights.

2 Insert rumex into hollow tips of horsetails.

3 Add caladium slanting right front.

60 cm (23½″)

C

A

B

Materials:
A: Fatsia japonica
B: Cockscomb
C: Grasstree

●Arranging Steps for 61:

1 Stand cockscomb so as not to show the stem.

2 Place fatsia leaves behind cockscomb, one in center, the other slanting right front.

3 Add grasstree behind, flowing left naturally.

TWO DESIGNS USING ONE CONTAINER

■ LARGE, SHALLOW CONTAINER: Use the water surface.

Container: H 4 cm × Diam 40 cm
(1½″ × 15½″)

Materials:
A: Veronica
B: Iris japonica leaf
C: Caladium
Kenzan (needlepoint holder)
Kansui-seki (marble-white pebbles)

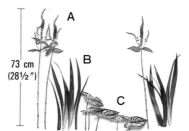
Right-side view of finished arrangement.

73 cm
(28½″)

● Arranging Steps:

Kansui-seki

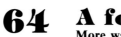

1 Stand veronica upright.

2 Add iris leaves to the base, flowing left.

3 Set caladium, varying the direction for each.

63 A focus on height.

Elegant veronica, reflected in the water. *Kansui-seki* (marble-white pebbles) lie at the bottom of the dish.

Finished size: H 76 cm × W 53 cm × D 58 cm
(29½″ × 20½″ × 22½″)

A

41 cm
(16″)

B

Materials:
A: Anthurium leaf
B: Hydrangea

● Arranging Steps:

Be sure the cut ends are well below the surface.

Fill with water.

Place hydrangea close to the base of leaves.

64 A focus on lowness.

More water, fewer flowers for a serene, cool look. Take the color of container into consideration.

Finished size: H 16 cm × W 46 cm × D 45 cm (6½″ × 18″ × 17½″)

Variation

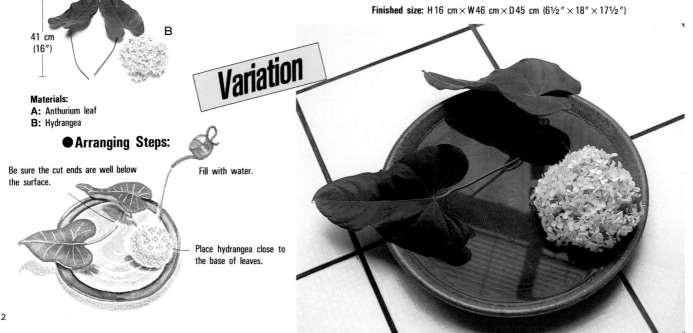

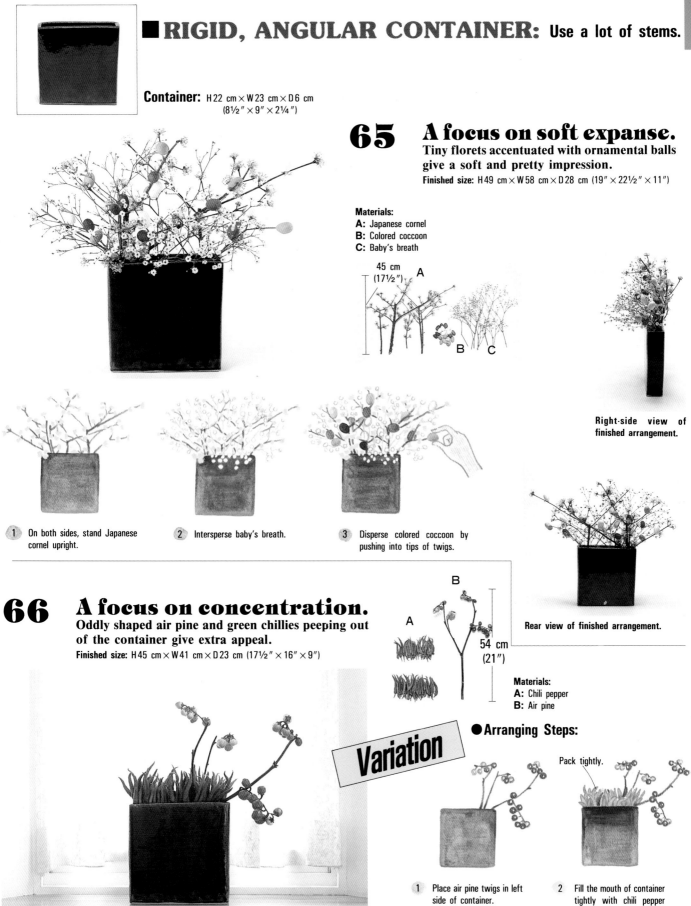

■RIGID, ANGULAR CONTAINER: Use a lot of stems.

Container: H 22 cm × W 23 cm × D 6 cm
(8½″ × 9″ × 2¼″)

65 A focus on soft expanse.

Tiny florets accentuated with ornamental balls give a soft and pretty impression.

Finished size: H 49 cm × W 58 cm × D 28 cm (19″ × 22½″ × 11″)

Materials:
A: Japanese cornel
B: Colored coccoon
C: Baby's breath

45 cm
(17½″) A

B C

Right-side view of finished arrangement.

1 On both sides, stand Japanese cornel upright.

2 Intersperse baby's breath.

3 Disperse colored coccoon by pushing into tips of twigs.

Rear view of finished arrangement.

66 A focus on concentration.

Oddly shaped air pine and green chillies peeping out of the container give extra appeal.

Finished size: H 45 cm × W 41 cm × D 23 cm (17½″ × 16″ × 9″)

B

A

54 cm
(21″)

Materials:
A: Chili pepper
B: Air pine

●Arranging Steps:

Variation

Pack tightly.

1 Place air pine twigs in left side of container.

2 Fill the mouth of container tightly with chili pepper pods.

53

ARRANGING WILD GRASSES

Wild grasses that bloom unnoticed in the field or roadside have unexpected charm and beauty if you look carefully. Arrange them in an informal container to bring nature into your home.

SEDUM & DRIED GRASS

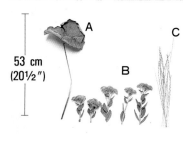

53 cm
(20½″)

Materials:
A: Dried lotus
B: Sedum erythrestictum
C: Dried grass

67

The density of sedum is lightened with a "fan" of dried lotus and wild grass.

Finished size: H 49 cm × W 58 cm × D 41 cm (19″ × 22½″ × 16″)

●Arranging Steps:

Right-side view of finished arrangement.

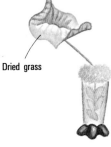

Container: Glass vase
H 20 cm × Diam 9 cm
(8″ × 3½″)

Dried grass

1 Set sedum to brim over rim. Slant lotus stalk left.

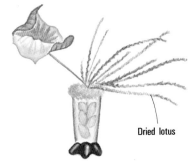

Dried lotus

2 Insert grass, from off-center towards right.

54

71
(27

Mat

Finished size: H 68 cm × W 68 cm × D 41 cm
(26½″ × 26½″ × 16″)

68 An amalgam of autumn colors and textures, spread widely for a wind-blown look.

Materials:
A: Great burnet
B: Foxtail
C: Cosmos

40 cm
(15½″)

A   B   C

Right-side view of finished arrangement.

Container: Cup

54 cm
(21″)

A   B

C

Materials:
A: Sanguisorba hakusanensis
B: Foxtail
C: Greenbrier

H 11 cm × Diam 7.5 cm
(4½″ × 3″)
Lay *kenzan* (needlepoint holder).

●Arranging Steps:

1 Set greenbrier.

2 Place foxtail slanting towards your right shoulder.

3 Add Sanguisorba to the center.

Container: Plant pot
H 11 cm × Diam 11 cm
(4½″ × 4½″)
Lay *kenzan* (needlepoint holder).

●Arranging Steps:

Slant the whole slightly forward.

1 Place great burnet cascading towards left. Add foxtail in radiation.

2 Position cosmos from center towards right.

69 A breezy, small cup arrangement will herald autumn.

Finished size: H 49 cm × W 45 cm × D 31 cm (19″ × 17½″ × 12″)

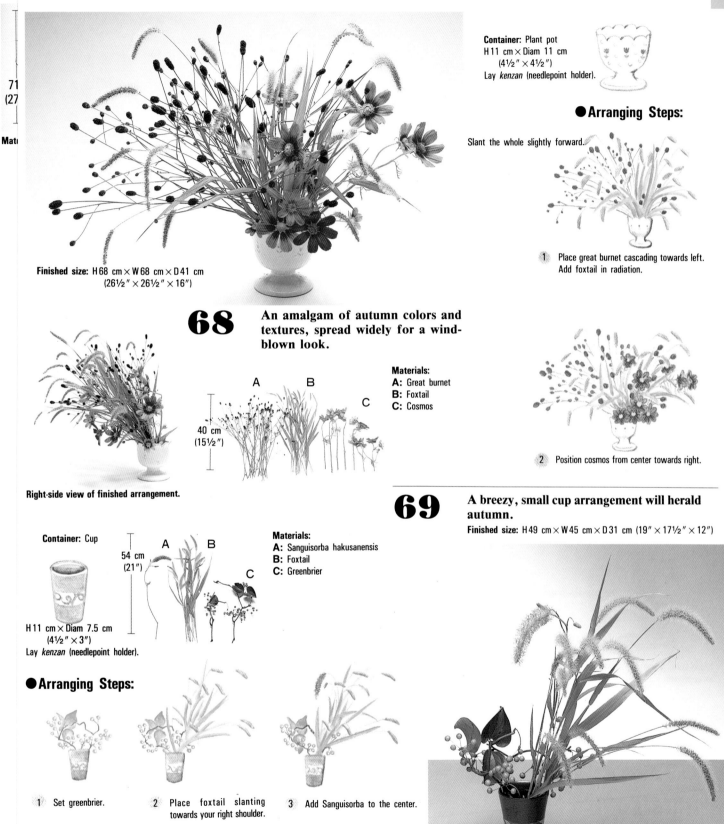

RUMEX

72

Rural charm; field grasses bring out the quiet colors of prairie gentian.

Finished size: H 49 cm × W 68 cm × D 49 cm
(19″ × 26½″ × 19″)

Left-side view of finished arrangement.

Materials:
A: Prairie gentian
B: Rosehip
C: Rumex

47 cm
(18¼″)

● Arranging Steps:

Rumex

Container:
Wooden wall container

H 14 cm × W 18 cm × D 7 cm
(5½″ × 7″ × 2½″)
Place a small vessel laid with *kenzan* (needlepoint holder).

Prairie gentian

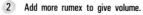

1. Place rosehip spreading to either side. Place longer stems of rumex slanting from center towards right.

2. Add more rumex to give volume.

3. Place prairie gentian in center.

PHYTOLACCA

Notice: Be careful when handling berries as they may leave stains on your hands or clothes if squashed.

73

Purple berries hang well when slanting the stem low. Natural foliage brings the field inside.

Finished size: H 41 cm × W 71 cm × D 46 cm (16″ × 27½″ × 18″)

Rear view of finished arrangement.

Left-side view of finished arrangement.

68 cm
(26½″)

Materials:
A: Phytolacca americana
B: Solidago altissima
C: Chrysanthemum

Container: Rattan basket

●Arranging Steps:

H 27 cm (including handle) × W 40 cm × D 28 cm
(10½″ × 15½″ × 11″)
Place a small vessel laid with *kenzan*
(needlepoint holder).

① Secure Phytolacca, slanting to either side.

② Add solidago and chrysanthemum so they bow to you.

CHRISTMAS

Beautifully illuminated streets always make you excited in this season. Arrange Christmas colors and brighten up your home.

74

A light-hearted, artistic display using red as the dominant color in contrast with green and white. Arrange as if drawing a picture in the air.

Materials: Poinsettia, Oncidium orchid, Smilax, Bleached golden apple, Wood glue
Container: Glass vase
Finished size: H 81 cm × W 63 cm × D 58 cm
(31½″ × 24½″ × 22½″)

See page 99 for arranging steps.

Red, green and white colors complement each other for a lively image.

75 **A whimsical arrangement in bright colors spills out from the matching vase.**
Materials: Baby's breath, Oncidium orchid, Smilax china, Falcatus
Container: Irregular-shaped vase
Finished size: H 63 cm × W 68 cm × D 49 cm (24½″ × 26½″ × 19″)
See page 98 for arranging steps.

CHRISTMAS

76

Tiny red ribbons give life to this fan-shaped arrangement of dried branches.
Materials: Bird-of-paradise, Cotton flower, Holly, Dried branch, Ribbon
Containers etc.: Irregular-shaped vase, *Kenzan* (needlepoint holder)
Finished size: H 51 cm × W 28 cm × D 31 cm (20″ × 11″ × 12″)
See page 104 for arranging steps.

Fill your home with flowers appropriately for the holiday season.

77

Silver-tinted asparagus fern will remind you of snowflakes. The focal point is a flaming red poinsettia.

Materials: Holly, Silver-tinted asparagus fern, Poinsettia, Glass ball ornament, #30 wire
Container: Grass vase
Finished size: H72 cm × W93 cm × D49 cm (29″ × 36½″ × 19″)
See page 106 for arranging steps.

78

A wreath on the door is always heartwarming. Here, dried apple slices are used to give homey look to a Christmas favorite.

Materials: Red vine, Filicoides aurea (variegated cedar), Eucaliptus, Smilax china, Dried apple slice, Ribbon, #30 wire
Finished size: Outside diam 40 cm (16″)
See page 107 for arranging steps.

THE NEW YEAR 79

Traditionally, the *tokonoma*, or alcove is decorated with pine arrangement, accompanied by round rice cakes in layers. Nowadays New Year arrangements are often displayed either at the entrance or in the living room.

Short-stemmed amaryllis flowers set off the beauty of long-needle pine tied with red *mizukihi* (paper cord).

Materials: Long-needle pine, Amaryllis, *Mizuhiki* (paper cord), #30 wire
Container: Glass vase
Finished size: H 72 cm × W 45 cm × D 40 cm (28″ × 17½″ × 15½″)
See page 104 for arranging steps.

Pine, a symbol of eternal life, can create a festive mood no matter what materials it is combined with.

80

It is said that the Goddess of Spring dwells in pine trees and brings happiness and good fortune in the coming year.

Materials: Young pine, Calla lily, Chrysanthemum
Containers etc.: Square vase, *Kenzan* (needlepoint holder)
Finished size: H 76 cm × W 53 cm × D 46 cm
(29½″ × 20½″ × 18″)
See page 106 for arranging steps.

81

Straw rope, woven in the traditional, religious way looped and decorated with symbols of good luck.

Materials: Pine, Pine cone, Ear of rice, *Mizuhiki* (paper cord), Crane-shaped *mizuhiki* ornament, Straw rope, #30 wire
Finished size: L 40 cm × W 16 cm (15½″ × 6½″)
See page 108 for arranging steps.

THE NEW YEAR

82 The strong lines of pine and lichened plum contrast with the delicacy of glory lilies and lace flowers. The golden weeping willow further enhances the festive mood.

Materials: Long-needle pine, Variegated pine, Glory lily, Lichened plum, Lace flower, Gilded weeping willow
Container: Vase
Finished size: H 96 cm × W 136 cm × D 87 cm (37½″ × 53″ × 34″)
See page 111 for arranging steps.

Make a regal arrangement for the *tokonoma*, or alcove.

83 To create an elegant mood, ensure the balance of color.

Materials: Variegated pine, White plum, Oncidium orchid, Chloranthus glaber, Bamboo stalk, *Washi* paper, Paper glue

Containers etc.: Rectangular *suiban* (shallow container), *Kenzan* (needlepoint holder)

Finished size: H 87 cm × W 93 cm × D 60 cm (34″ × 36½″ × 23½″)

See page 110 for arranging steps.

DOLL FESTIVAL

The doll festival is a celebration held on March 3 when households with daughters display a set of traditional dolls. They wish for strong, healthy daughters. The dolls are accompanied by special rice cakes, *sake*, and peach blossoms which are believed to protect little girls from harm.

84   **In a display of peach blossoms, vivid colors create a festive mood.**
Materials: Peach blossom, Mimosa, Tulip, Spirea
Container: Square vase
Finished size: H 46 cm × W 82 cm × D 53 cm (18″ × 32″ × 20½″)
See page 108 for arranging steps.

Cheerful arrangements with best wishes for your little girls.

85

This arrangement includes small decorations for fun such as a pair of shells with paintings of ancient emperor and empress.

Materials: Golden bell, Peach blossom, Fennel, Baby's breath
Containers: 2 glasses, Small dish
Finished size: H 31 cm × W 58 cm (12″ × 22½″)

● **Arranging Steps:**

Put the containers in a line. Arrange fennel in the small dish, in a dome shape. Slant golden bell in the middle container. In the short tumbler, place baby's breath.

★ **How to fold a paper doll:**

18 cm
(7″)

Origami (colored side)

What you need:
2 sheets *origami*
Sweet pea
Ear of barley

Outer fold

1 Fold in half.

2 Fold again in half.

3 Bring ends over.

Bring up top two layers.   Insert a flower.

4 Fold ends down.

86

Cute *origami* dolls put in front of the flowers have flower "heads", which will excite the children at the party.

Materials: Peach blossom, Golden bell, Baby's breath
Containers etc.: Lacquered measuring cup, *Kenzan* (needlepoint holder)
Finished size: H 40 cm × W 53 cm × D 34 cm (15½″ × 20½″ × 13½″)

See page 109 for arranging steps.

BOYS' DAY

This is a festival for boys held on May 5 when families with sons fly carp streamers and display armor in the hope that their little sons will grow up strong. Sweetflag is a must for this festival.

87   A sweetflag leaf symbolizes a sword. Show the upright stance of the leaves accented with billberry, suggesting a breeze.

Materials: Sweetflag, Billberry

Containers etc.: Round *suiban* (shallow container), *Kenzan* (needlepoint holder), *Kansui-seki* (marble-white pebbles)

Finished size: H 72 cm × W 68 cm × D 55 cm (28″ × 26½″ × 21½″)

See page 112 for arranging steps.

Make a straight and tall display in the way the boy will grow.

88

Beautifully fanned out iris leaves express gentleness. Kakitsu iris represents the growth of girls, while sweetflag represents boys.

Materials: Kakitsu iris, Privet
Container: Irregular-shaped vase
Finished size: H 63 cm × W 63 cm × D 50 cm
(24½″ × 24½″ × 19½″)

See page 105 for arranging steps.

89

Miniature weapons made for dolls make effective accessories in a tall arrangement of Japanese yew.

Materials: Japanese yew, Miniature bow, arrows, and spear
Container: Single-flower vase
Finished size: H 63 cm × W 35 cm × D 27 cm (24½″ × 13½″ × 10½″)

● **Arranging Steps:**
Stand the Japanese yew securely. Decorate with miniature bow, arrows and spear.

MOTHER'S DAY

For the second Sunday of May, why don't you make a flower arrangement instead of just a plain bouquet? Fill the room with sweet carnations of your choice.

90 Carnations and baby's breath radiate from the rose-tinted lilies, the focal point. A stemmed vase completes a feminine image.

Materials: Carnation, Baby's breath, Lily
Containers etc.: Stemmed vase, *Kenzan* (needlepoint holder)
Finished size: H 50 cm × W 73 cm × D 41 cm (19½″ × 28½″ × 16″)
See page 115 for arranging steps.

Express your thanks with an original arrangement of flowers.

91 A gift of flowers rearranged into a display with style.

Materials: Carnation, Spray carnation, Baby's breath, Leather fern
Container: Glass vase
Finished size: H 58 cm × W 64 cm × D 50 cm
         (22½" × 25" × 19½")
See page 114 for arranging steps.

STAR FESTIVAL

According to a Chinese legend, on the eve of July 7, the Weaver Star Princess is allowed to meet her love, the Herdboy Star on the bank of the Milky Way. It is said that if you write your wishes on strips of colored paper and hang them on a bamboo tree on this night, your dreams will come true.

92 Trim the bamboo branches by removing some leaves to show the definite lines. Strings of five colors symbolize the ties between the lovers as well as the wishes hanging from the bamboo.

Materials: Bamboo, Lily, Colored strings (red, yellow, white, navy, black), #30 wire
Container: Tube-shaped vase
Finished size: H 82 cm × W 76 cm × D 60 cm (32″ × 29½″ × 23½″)
See page 105 for arranging steps.

MOON-VIEWING PARTY

On the fifteenth night of August by the lunar calendar, the full moon was admired as the harvest moon. Today, in the middle of September, we still enjoy the moon with rice dumplings and the seven autumnal flowers.

93

An autumn field is reproduced with a natural but careful assortment in a large basket, in which green briar vine idly rests.

Materials: Japanese pampas, Polygonum orientale, Great burnet, Patrinia scabiosafolia, Helenium, Cockscomb, Greenbriar

Containers etc.: Basket, Small vessel, *Kenzan* (needlepoint holder)

Finished size: H 73 cm × W 76 cm × D 73 cm
(28½″ × 29½″ × 28½″)

See page 113 for arranging steps.

BIRTHDAY

For your own or someone else's birthday, express your joy by creating a display full of personality

94 The soft flowing lines of spirea at two levels develop a theme along with the pastel flowers.

Materials: Spirea, Rose, Paper bush
Container: Irregular-shaped vase
Finished size: H 72 cm × W 77 cm × D 59 cm (28″ × 28″ × 23″)
See page 114 for arranging steps.

Make the birthday arrangement buoyant and cheerful to reflect happiness.

95

The contrast between the thin spiky branch and the voluminous flowers gives this arrangement dramatic impact.

Materials: Amaryllis, Iris japonica leaf, Dried briar
Container: Glass vase
Finished size: H 91 cm × W 63 cm × D 63 cm
(35½″ × 24½″ × 24½″)
See page 116 for arranging steps.

96

Once in a while, do something different. Here, the beautiful variegated leaves are enlarged by a lens of water.

Materials: Rose, Miniature rose, Dieffenbachia
Container: Glass vase
Finished size: H 45 cm × W 64 cm × D 40 cm
(17½″ × 25″ × 15½″)
See page 116 for arranging steps.

MASTERING BASIC STYLES

Although ikebana seems to include numerous forms or designs, each arrangement is an interpretation of three basic styles: "Slanting", "Upright", and "Cascading" styles. Mastering these styles is essential for you to discover the most beautiful shapes of the flowers, and realize your own creativity.

SLANTING STYLE - Arranging in *suiban* (shallow container)

Set the dominant curvy stem first. Then pick a thinner, shorter one to slant in the opposite direction. The distance between these stems creates a space.

97 A delightful atmosphere is achieved by soft tone flowers arranged in a very basic way.
Finished size: H50 cm × W72 cm × D40 cm (19½″ × 28″ × 15½″)

Materials:
A: Japanese cornel
B: Rose

68 cm
(26½")

A

B

34 cm
(13")

a   b   c

Container:
Suiban (shallow container)
H 10 cm × D 18 cm × W 23 cm (4" × 7" × 9")
Lay *kenzan* (needlepoint holder).

How to decide lengths of main stems:

Width

Height

Container

$\phi = $ Width + Height of container

$a = \phi \times 1\frac{1}{2}$ (approx.)
$b = a \times \frac{3}{4}$ (approx.)
$c = b \times \frac{1}{2}$ to $\frac{3}{4}$ (approx.)

a

b

c

Stem (**a**)   Center   Stem (**b**)

Flower (**c**)

View from above:

a

b

c

Check the Shape

Front view of finished arrangement. Note how flexibly the branches stretch.

Rear view of finished arrangement. Japanese cornel branches create depth.

Left-side view of finished arrangement.

Right-side view of finished arrangement. The roses slant low forward.

● Arranging Steps:

① Position *kenzan* at back right of container. Place Japanese cornel (**a**), slanting left to about 45°.

② Place Japanese cornel at center, slanting back right to about 10° to 15°.

③ Two main branches (**a** & **b**) are secured in *kenzan*.

④ Place rose (**c**) slanting very low, about 75° towards your right shoulder.

⑤ Add more roses slanting forward.

⑥ Fill back and front with more twigs of Japanese cornel to finish up.

UPRIGHT STYLE - Arranging in a tall vase

The main branch is placed to create a clean, upright line. Make the arrangement near and compact at the neck of the vase.

98

Beautiful streamlined red-budding willow enhanced with delicate tone prairie gentian, for a gentle warmth.
Finished size: H 96 cm × W 63 cm × D 50 cm (37½″ × 24½″ × 19½″)

Materials:
A: Red-budding willow
B: Prairie gentian

81 cm
(31½")

34 cm
(13")

a   b   c

Container:
Tube-shaped vase
H 31 cm × Diam 9 cm
(12" × 3½")

How to decide lengths of main stems:

Diameter

a

b

c

Container

ϕ = Width + Height of container

a = ϕ × 1½ to 2 (approx.)
b = **a** × ¾ (approx.)
c = **b** × ½ to ¾ (approx.)

MAKING A SPLINT

Center

Stem (**a**)

Stem (**b**)

Flower (**c**)

View from above:

a

b

c

Note that the lengths do not include the stems within the vase. Cut the materials to adjust your container.

① Cut the supporting stalk a little shorter than the height of the vase. Split the end to the determined length.

② Split the end of willow (**a**) and interlock with the split end of supporting stalk.

③ Adjust the angle to fit the vase.

Check the Shape

Front view of finished arrangement. Branches extend freely upward and forward.

Right-side view of finished arrangement. Note how the flowers protrude.

Rear view of finished arrangement.

Left-side view of finished arrangement.

● Arranging Steps:

① Put red-budding willow (**a**) fixed to the splint as above, slanting a little left to about 10° to 15°.

② Add willow (**b**) slanting lower, to about 45°.

③ Hold prairie gentian (**c**) facing towards your right shoulder and set at about 75°.

④ Now stems (**a**) (**b**) (**c**) are in position.

⑤ Add more prairie gentians to center, slanting forward.

⑥ Finish with willow twigs, adding to back and left of (**a**).

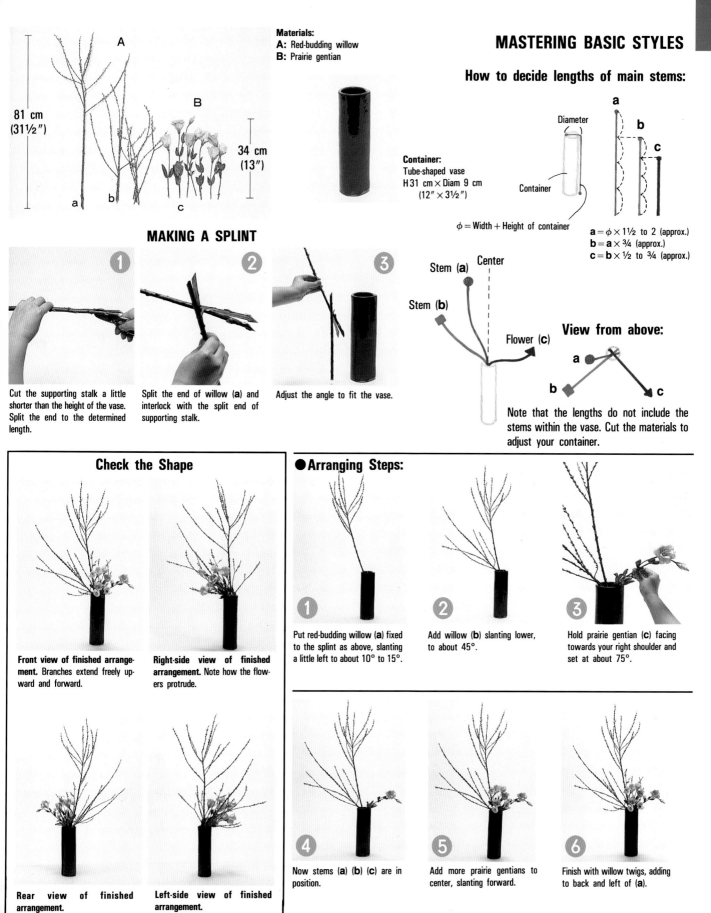

CASCADING STYLE - Arranging in a tall vase

In this style the main stem is set lower than the rim of the vase. Choose a branch which has beautiful natural curves.

The colors and textures of leaves and flowers contrast well with the tall black vase.
Finished size: H 53 cm × W 64 cm × D 45 cm (20½″ × 25″ × 17½″)

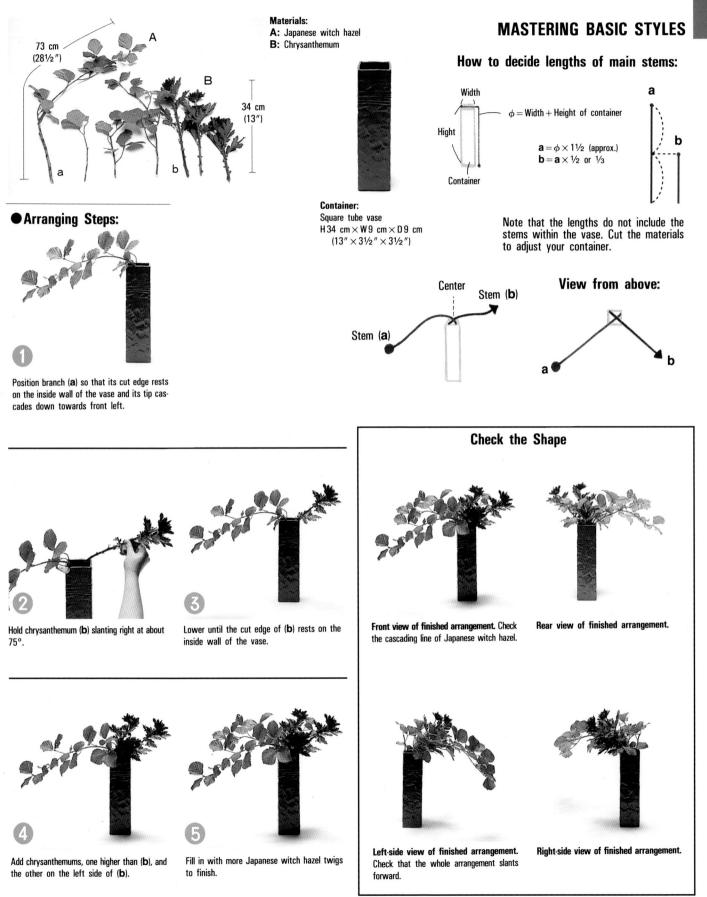

Materials:
A: Japanese witch hazel
B: Chrysanthemum

73 cm (28½″)

34 cm (13″)

A

B

a

b

Container:
Square tube vase
H 34 cm × W 9 cm × D 9 cm
(13″ × 3½″ × 3½″)

How to decide lengths of main stems:

Width

Hight

Container

ϕ = Width + Height of container

$a = \phi \times 1\frac{1}{2}$ (approx.)
$b = a \times \frac{1}{2}$ or $\frac{1}{3}$

a

b

Note that the lengths do not include the stems within the vase. Cut the materials to adjust your container.

Center

Stem (b)

Stem (a)

View from above:

a

b

● Arranging Steps:

1 Position branch (a) so that its cut edge rests on the inside wall of the vase and its tip cascades down towards front left.

2 Hold chrysanthemum (b) slanting right at about 75°.

3 Lower until the cut edge of (b) rests on the inside wall of the vase.

4 Add chrysanthemums, one higher than (b), and the other on the left side of (b).

5 Fill in with more Japanese witch hazel twigs to finish.

Check the Shape

Front view of finished arrangement. Check the cascading line of Japanese witch hazel.

Rear view of finished arrangement.

Left-side view of finished arrangement. Check that the whole arrangement slants forward.

Right-side view of finished arrangement.

1 on page 6

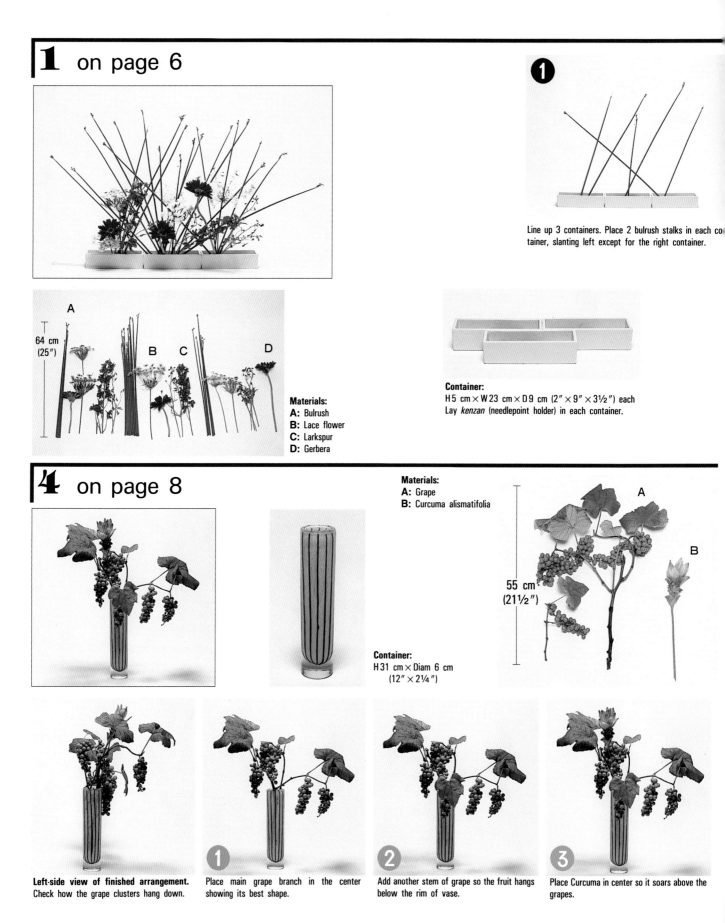

①

Line up 3 containers. Place 2 bulrush stalks in each container, slanting left except for the right container.

64 cm
(25″)

A

B   C

D

Materials:
A: Bulrush
B: Lace flower
C: Larkspur
D: Gerbera

Container:
H 5 cm × W 23 cm × D 9 cm (2″ × 9″ × 3½″) each
Lay *kenzan* (needlepoint holder) in each container.

4 on page 8

Materials:
A: Grape
B: Curcuma alismatifolia

A

B

55 cm
(21½″)

Container:
H 31 cm × Diam 6 cm
(12″ × 2¼″)

Left-side view of finished arrangement.
Check how the grape clusters hang down.

① Place main grape branch in the center showing its best shape.

② Add another stem of grape so the fruit hangs below the rim of vase.

③ Place Curcuma in center so it soars above the grapes.

❷

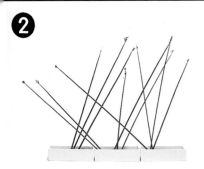

Add more stalks checking the balance.

❸

Now the bulrush stalks are fanned out.

❹

Place larkspur slanting in line with bulrush.

❺

Add more larkspur to the front.

❻

Place lace flower in each container as appropriate.

❼

Place gerberas in left and center containers slanting forward.

5 on page 9

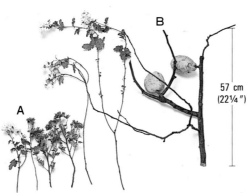

Materials:
A: Spray mum
(in variety of colors)
B: Chinese quince

57 cm
(22¼")

Left-side view of finished arrangement.
Check how the thin branches are slanting
forward.

Container:
H 37 cm × Diam 9 cm
(14½" × 3½")

❶ Stand Chinese quince in center.

❷ Place yellow mum slanting horizontally
towards front left.

❸ Stand white mum upright slightly higher
than the fruits.

❹ Finish off by adding pink mum low to
cover the rim of vase.

3 on page 7

Container:
H 5 cm × D 16 cm × W 20 cm
(2″ × 6½″ × 8″)

Materials:
A: Yellow-leaf spirea
B: Camellia

1 Lay a small vessel lined with *kenzan* inside the basket. Center yellow-leaf spirea slanting left.

2 Take a shorter branch and place in center, slanting low towards front right.

3 Fill in with more spirea twigs to conceal the inner container.

4 Stand camellia upright in center.

---

9 on page 12

Container: H 22 cm × W 27 cm
(8½″ × 10½″)

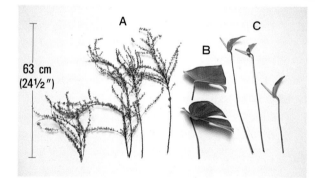

Materials: **A:** Spirea (pink)
B: Monstera
C: Anthurium

1 Place spirea in left and right openings so they cross each other.

2 Place another branch upright in the left side of container.

3 Add more spirea to the left side for volume.

4 Put Monstera stem in the right side facing front and leaning right.

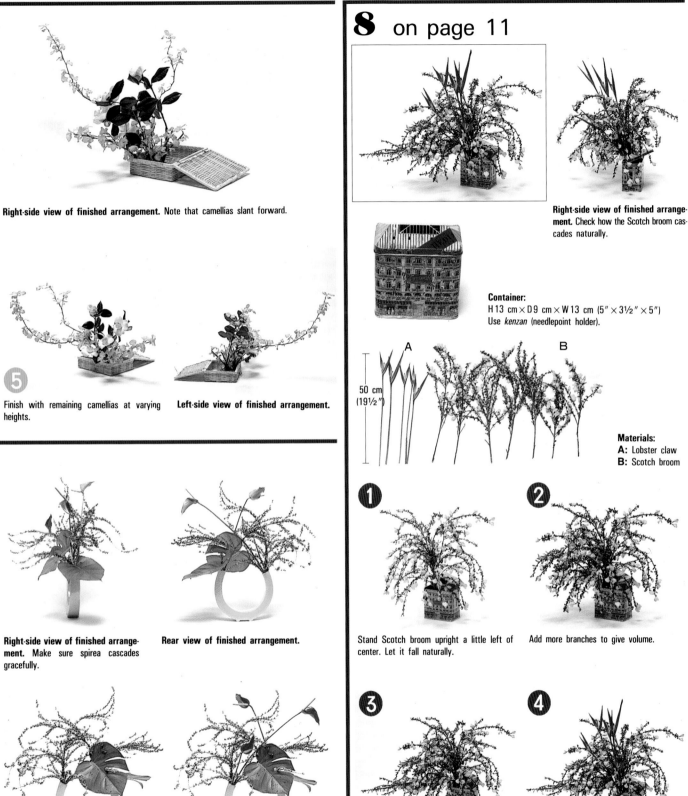

Right-side view of finished arrangement. Note that camellias slant forward.

⑤ Finish with remaining camellias at varying heights.

Left-side view of finished arrangement.

Right-side view of finished arrangement. Make sure spirea cascades gracefully.

Rear view of finished arrangement.

⑤ Place other leaf behind, horizontally.

⑥ Insert two anthuriums, one in each side and cross over. Add a shorter stem to the left, slanting forward.

8 on page 11

Right-side view of finished arrangement. Check how the Scotch broom cascades naturally.

Container:
H 13 cm × D 9 cm × W 13 cm (5″ × 3½″ × 5″)
Use *kenzan* (needlepoint holder).

50 cm
(19½″)

A   B

Materials:
A: Lobster claw
B: Scotch broom

① Stand Scotch broom upright a little left of center. Let it fall naturally.

② Add more branches to give volume.

③ Secure 1 straight branch slanting left horizontally.

④ Place lobster claw in center, slanting a little towards your left shoulder.

87

28 on page 25

Materials: A: Glory lily
B: Sunflower
C: Smilax

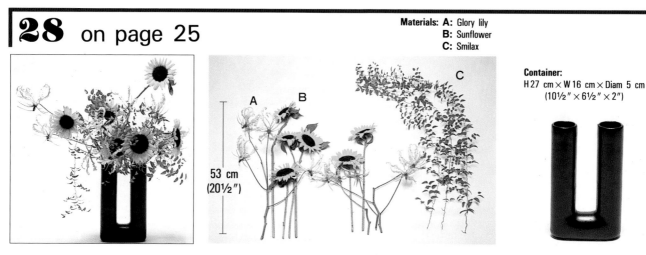

Container:
H 27 cm × W 16 cm × Diam 5 cm
(10½″ × 6½″ × 2″)

53 cm
(20½″)

①
Put 2 sunflowers in the left opening, leaning in opposite ways.

②
Put a short sunflower in left opening, and slightly longer one to the right so they partly overlap.

③
Stand one more upright in left. Place another in right, facing outward.

④
Add lily in front and behind sunflowers.

29 on page 26

Container:
H 13 cm × W 37 cm × D 22 cm
(5″ × 14½″ × 8½″)

Right-side view of finished arrangement.

①
Place fern fronds so they spread horizontally to sides.

45 cm
(17½″)

Materials: A: Scabiosa japonica
B: Baby's breath
C: Miniature rose
D: Leather fern

③
Use baby's breath in right opening to form an asymmetrical cloud.

④
Put baby's breath in left opening also.

Rear view of finished arrangement, with sunflowers facing forward.

Left-side view of finished arrangement.

⑤ Insert smilax vines to hang over the flowers.

⑥ Finished arrangement.

② Put miniature rose low in both openings.

⑤ Insert a short Scabiosa facing forward. Add taller Scabiosa slanting left and right.

10 on page 12

Container:
H 16 cm × W 32 cm × D 2.5 cm
(6½″ × 12½″ × 1″)

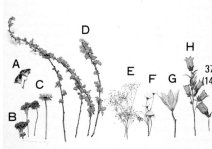

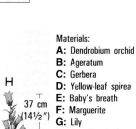

37 cm
(14½″)

Materials:
A: Dendrobium orchid
B: Ageratum
C: Gerbera
D: Yellow-leaf spirea
E: Baby's breath
F: Marguerite
G: Lily
H: Cantabury-bells

① Slant yellow-leaf spirea right so the cut end touches the left bottom. Then center another stem and lean on opposite side.

② Place another stem starting from the right bottom, flowing naturally left.

③ Stand Cantabury-bells on the right.

④ Stand gerbera upright on the left, ageratum in center.

⑤ Insert lily between gerbera and ageratum, orchid between ageratum and Cantabury-bells.

⑥ Finish off with marguerite on the very left, baby's breath on the right side.

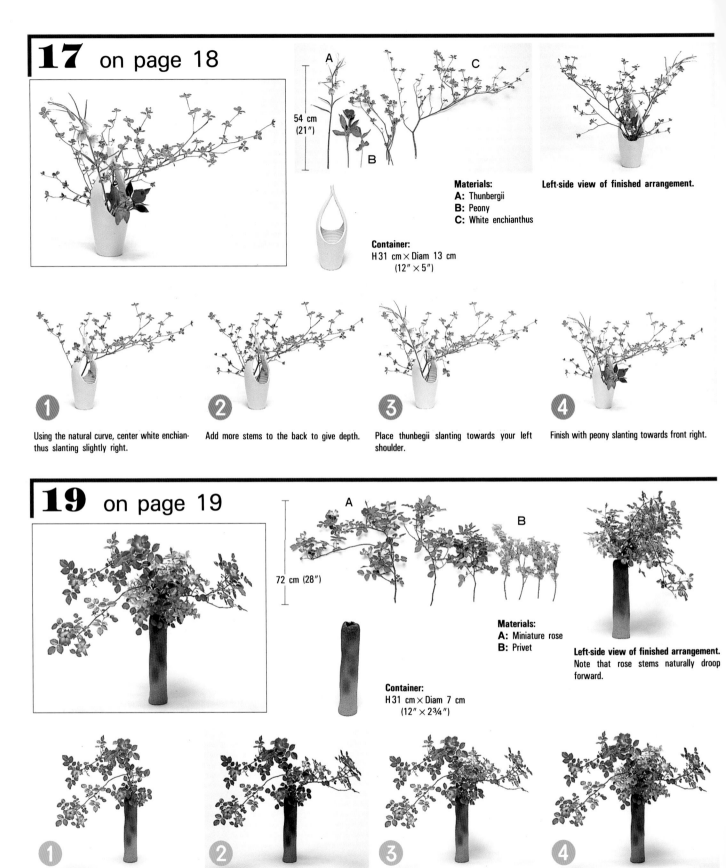

17 on page 18

54 cm (21")

Materials:
A: Thunbergii
B: Peony
C: White enchianthus

Container:
H 31 cm × Diam 13 cm
(12" × 5")

Left-side view of finished arrangement.

1 Using the natural curve, center white enchianthus slanting slightly right.

2 Add more stems to the back to give depth.

3 Place thunbegii slanting towards your left shoulder.

4 Finish with peony slanting towards front right.

19 on page 19

72 cm (28")

Materials:
A: Miniature rose
B: Privet

Container:
H 31 cm × Diam 7 cm
(12" × 2¾")

Left-side view of finished arrangement.
Note that rose stems naturally droop forward.

1 Stand rose upright so the branches fall naturally towards left.

2 Place another stem to rise in the opposite direction.

3 Add more rose to fill in center.

4 Finish off by inserting privet stems in center and back, slanting forward.

20 on page 20

28 cm
(11")

Materials: Hydrangea

Left-side view of finished arrangement. Note that the center of gravity is in the front.

Container:
H 27 cm, Inner diam 5 cm (10½", 2")

① Place 2 hydrangeas slanting almost horizontally in both directions.

② Add the shortest stem to center, facing forward.

③ Frame the central flower by putting a stem of leaves behind.

24 on page 23

Container:
H 10 cm, Opening diam 9 cm (4", 3½")

A   B

42 cm
(16¼")

Materials:
A: Astilbe
B: Gerbera

Rear view of finished arrangement. Note how many flowers are used to give depth.

① Place yellow gerbera low in center. Put several more around it, in varying heights.

② Add more gerberas to right back, standing upright.

③ Place Astilbe in back of arrangement, slanting a little left.

④ Add more to right back to act as a foil to the gerberas.

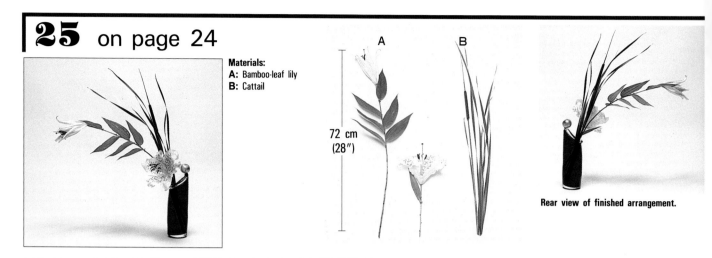

Materials:
A: Bamboo-leaf lily
B: Cattail

72 cm
(28")

Rear view of finished arrangement.

Container:
H 28 cm × Diam 7 cm (11" × 2¾")

① Holding a long stemmed lily, slant forward with cut edge resting on the inside of the vase.

② Set a short-stemmed lily slanting a little forward.

③ Place cattail behind to flow over the long-stemmed lily.

---

26 on page 24

A   B

54 cm
(21")

Materials:
A: Smokegrass
B: Stomona japonica

Right-side view of finished arrangement.

Container:
H 27 cm, Inner diam 14 cm (10½", 5½")

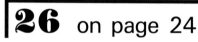

① Using the natural curve, set a stem of Stomona japonica so its cut edge rests on the inside of the vase.

② Add another stem slanting right horizontally.

③ Add more to cover the rim of vase, cascading forward.

④ Place smokegrass slanting from back left to front for the finished arrangement.

27 on page 25

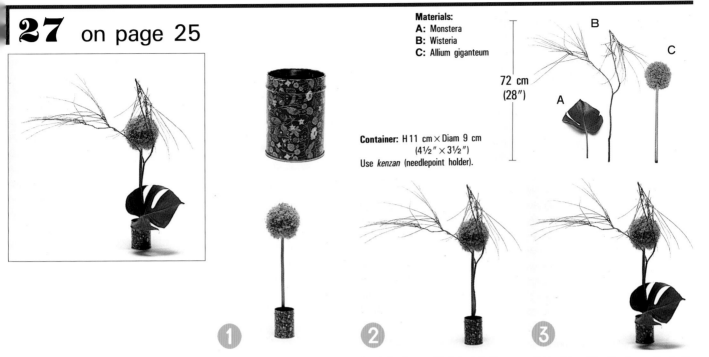

Materials:
A: Monstera
B: Wisteria
C: Allium giganteum

72 cm (28")

Container: H 11 cm × Diam 9 cm (4½" × 3½")
Use *kenzan* (needlepoint holder).

① Stand allium upright in center.

② Stand wisteria stem right in front of allium so the stems look like a single vertical line.

③ Finish off by adding Monstera so the tip of leaf points to right.

37 on page 31

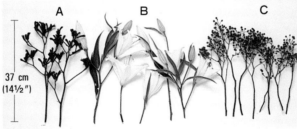

Rear view of finished arrangement.
Check the overall depth and the round form of kangaroo paw and rosehip.

Materials:
A: Kangaroo paw
B: Lily
C: Rosehip
30 wire

37 cm (14½")

Container:
H 18 cm,
Opening diam 18 cm
(7", 7")

① Hold 3 stems of lily in varying lengths, and wire just below the flower heads.

② Position wired lilies at center right. Add remaining lilies.

③ Place rosehip in a round shape.

④ Finish off by putting kangaroo paw to back left.

30 on page 27

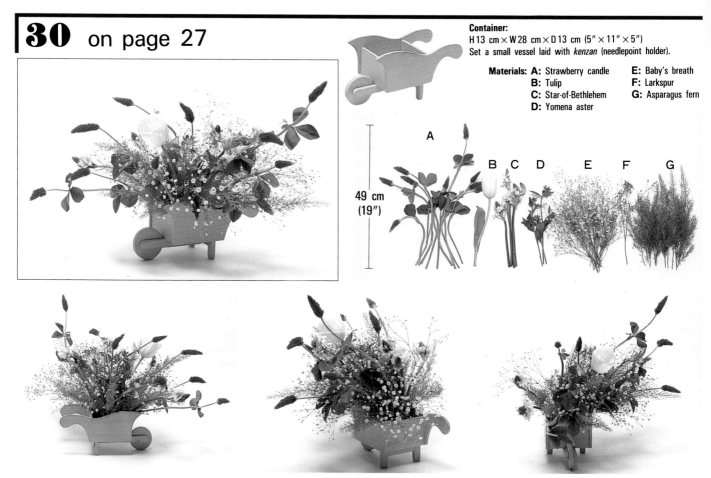

Container:
H 13 cm × W 28 cm × D 13 cm (5″ × 11″ × 5″)
Set a small vessel laid with *kenzan* (needlepoint holder).

Materials: **A:** Strawberry candle   **E:** Baby's breath
           B: Tulip   **F:** Larkspur
           C: Star-of-Bethlehem   **G:** Asparagus fern
           D: Yomena aster

49 cm
(19″)

Rear view of finished arrangement. Check the directions of asparagus.

Right-side view of finished arrangement.

Left-side view of finished arrangement with most flowers.

① Place 2 long stems of strawberry candle slanting low towards both sides.

② Add more strawberry candles in varying heights to form a fan shape.

③ Place tulip at center left, slanting front left.

④ Place star-of-Bethlehem in front right and left.

⑤ Center yomena asters and larkspur.

⑥ Place asparagus fern low in radiation.

⑦ Finish off by adding baby's breath spreading throughout the arrangement.

31 on page 27

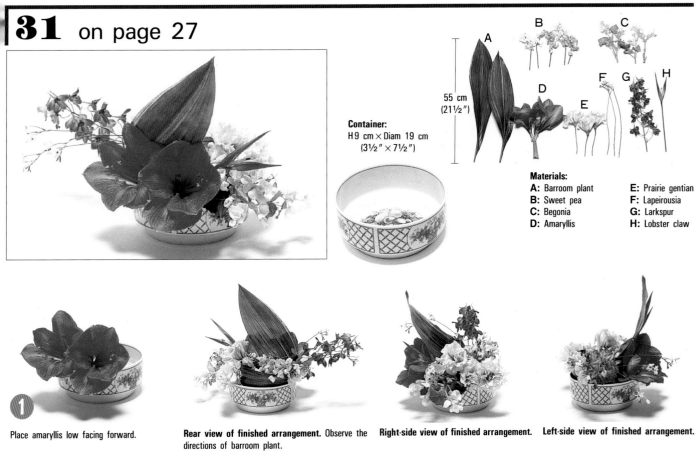

Container:
H 9 cm × Diam 19 cm
(3½" × 7½")

55 cm
(21½")

Materials:
A: Barroom plant **E:** Prairie gentian
B: Sweet pea **F:** Lapeirousia
C: Begonia **G:** Larkspur
D: Amaryllis **H:** Lobster claw

Place amaryllis low facing forward.

Rear view of finished arrangement. Observe the directions of barroom plant.

Right-side view of finished arrangement.

Left-side view of finished arrangement.

Curl barroom plant leaf along the inner wall of the container, starting from right.

Now the leaf is set inside the container.

Stand another leaf on left, slanting towards right.

Place begonia horizontally in right.

Place sweet pea in back right, sticking well over begonia.

Put prairie gentian slanting a little backward.

Place larkspur in back slanting left.

Finally put lobster claw behind amaryllis, and Lapeirousia in front of larkspur.

35 on page 30

Materials:
A: African lily
B: Billberry
C: Cattail
D: Super lady

100 cm (39″)

A B C D

Container:
H 27 cm × Diam 16 cm
(10½″ × 6½″)

① Place billberry slanting left showing the natural curve.

② Add another branch slanting forward as far as possible.

Rear view of finished arrangement.

Right-side view of finished arrangement. Note the whole arrangement slants forward.

③ Place super lady in right front, slanting low.

④ Place African lily facing front right.

⑤ Put cattail in back left, slanting naturally forward.

⑥ Add more cattail to center.

75 on page 61

A B C D

55 cm (21½″)

Materials:
A: Smilax china
B: Falcatus
C: Baby's breath
D: Oncidium orchid

Container:
H 32 cm × W 11 cm × D 4 cm
(12½″ × 4″ × 1½″)

Rear view of finished arrangement. Note the fluffy expansion of baby's breath.

Right-side view of finished arrangement.

74 on page 60

Materials:
A: Bleached golden apple
B: Poinsettia
C: Oncidium orchid
D: Smilax
Wood glue

68 cm
(26½")

① Make a lattice by arranging bleached branches at random and gluing together.

Container:
H 23 cm, Opening diam 9 cm (9″, 3½″)

Rear view of finished arrangement. Note that the lattice is encircled by smilax vine.

Right-side view of finished arrangement. Notice how the poinsettia slants forward.

② Stand the lattice in the center of vase.

③ Using a long smilax vine, make an arch as shown.

④ Fix end of vine to lattice as shown.

⑤ Insert poinsettia slanting forward in center.

⑥ Stand orchid upright behind the lattice to finish.

① Place Falcatus to cascade towards left.

② Place another Falcatus stem right.

③ Center orchid slanting forward.

④ Insert baby's breath to form a fluffy cloud.

⑤ Insert smilax china to cascade towards front left.

38 on page 32

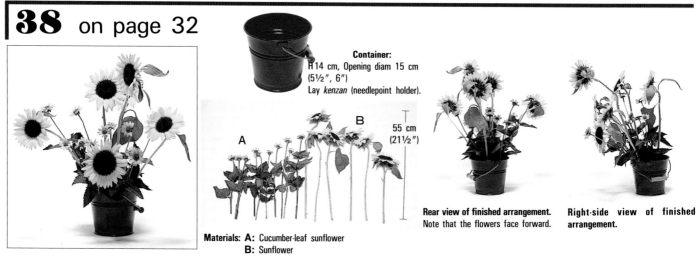

Container:
H 14 cm, Opening diam 15 cm
(5½″, 6″)
Lay *kenzan* (needlepoint holder).

A

B

55 cm
(21½″)

Materials: A: Cucumber-leaf sunflower
B: Sunflower

Rear view of finished arrangement. Note that the flowers face forward.

Right-side view of finished arrangement.

1 Put two sunflowers, one in center, one on left, both facing front.

2 Center a long stem facing left. Place a shorter stem at right.

3 Add 2 more sunflowers, one right, one center. Add cucumber-leaf sunflowers starting from center as far as left.

4 Add more cucumber-leaf sunflowers recessing low.

40 on page 33

76 cm
(29½″)

A

B

C

D

Materials: A: Verbena tenera   **C:** Alocasia
B: Baby's breath   **D:** Monstera

Rear view of finished arrangement.

Right-side view of finished arrangement.

Container:

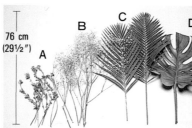

H 27 cm,
Opening diam 16 cm
(10½″, 6½″)

1 Put Monstera in center, slanting right.

2 Place Alocasia in the front, pointing left.

3 Place baby's breath slanting forward.

4 Disperse verbena tenera within baby's breath.

44 on page 36

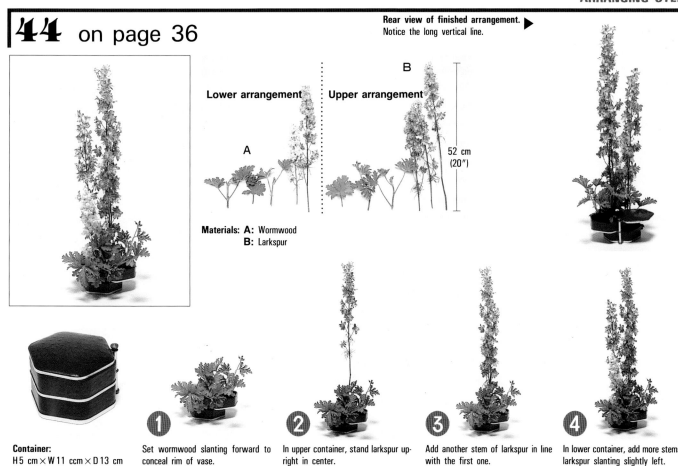

Lower arrangement

A

Upper arrangement

B

52 cm
(20″)

Materials: A: Wormwood
B: Larkspur

Container:
H 5 cm × W 11 ccm × D 13 cm
(2″ × 4½″ × 5″)

① Set wormwood slanting forward to conceal rim of vase.

② In upper container, stand larkspur upright in center.

③ Add another stem of larkspur in line with the first one.

④ In lower container, add more stems of larkspur slanting slightly left.

46 on page 37

① Put lilac so branches slant towards left and right.

② Place a short stem of lilac, nestling close to the left-side branch.

③ Add more twigs protruding forward to conceal rim of vase.

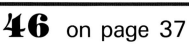

A

B

36 cm
(14″)

Materials: A: Prairie gentian
B: Lilac

Container:
H 9 cm × Diam 9 cm
(3½″ × 3½″)

④ Place prairie gentian in center slanting forward.

⑤ Add longer stems of prairie gentian to back left to finish.

43 on page 35

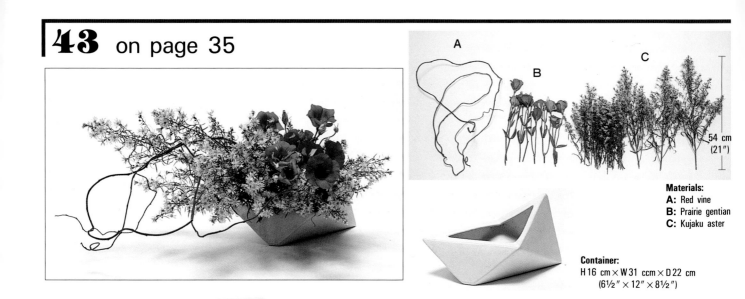

Materials:
A: Red vine
B: Prairie gentian
C: Kujaku aster

Container:
H 16 cm × W 31 ccm × D 22 cm
(6½" × 12" × 8½")

54 cm
(21")

A

B

C

Rear view of finished arrangement.

Right-side view of finished arrangement.

Left-side view of finished arrangement. Notice the entwined vine.

1

Slant kujaku aster low towards left.

2

Add more aster so they protrude forward.

3

Add slightly shorter stems, slanting from center towards right.

4

Insert red vine low, hanging forward from center to left.

5

Insert another vine behind and bring it to front, drawing a circle.

6

Finally add prairie gentian in center slanting forward. (Be sure the vine does not touch the surface of table.)

48 on page 39

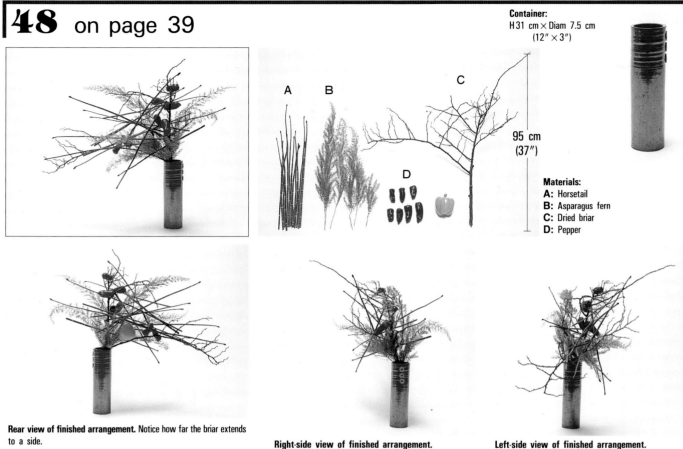

Container:
H 31 cm × Diam 7.5 cm
(12″ × 3″)

C

95 cm
(37″)

A B

D

Materials:
A: Horsetail
B: Asparagus fern
C: Dried briar
D: Pepper

Rear view of finished arrangement. Notice how far the briar extends to a side.

Right-side view of finished arrangement.

Left-side view of finished arrangement.

1 Stand briar upright in center.

2  Insert thorns of briar into peppers.

3  Yellow bell pepper is positioned near center, red pepper further out.

4 Attach more peppers onto vertical branch to make a good balance.

5  Secure horsetail stalks on thorns.

6  Attach more stalks in several directions to cross over each other.

7 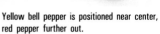 Put asparagus behind on the left, slanting left.

8  Finish by adding more fronds of asparagus to extend left and right.

76 on page 62

Container:
H 13 cm × W 19 cm × D 10 cm
(5″ × 7½″ × 4″)
Lay *kenzan* (needlepoint holder).

Decorate a fan-shaped dried branch with small ribbon bows and place behind the arrangement.

50 cm
(19½″)

100 cm (39″)

D

50 cm
(19½″)

A

B

C

Materials: A: Bird-of-paradise
B: Cotton flower
C: Holly
D: Dried branch

1 Stand cotton flowers upright in center, facing front.

2 Stand bird-of-paradise behind, facing left.

3 Place holly below the cotton flowers. Add a longer stem behind.

Rear view of finished arrangement.

Right-side view of finished arrangement. Notice the vertical line of bird-of-paradise.

79 on page 64

Materials:
A: Amaryllis
B: Long-needle pine
C: *Mizuhiki* (paper cord)
30 wire

Container:
H 31 cm, Opening diam 6 cm (12″, 2¼″)

72 cm
(28″)

A

B

C

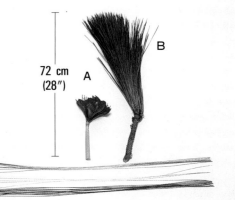

1 Bind the base of pine needles with *mizuhiki*.

2 Holding ends of *mizuhiki* upward, secure with wire.

3 Place pine in the vase, slanting left.

4 Finish with amaryllis concealing rim of vase.

88 on page 71

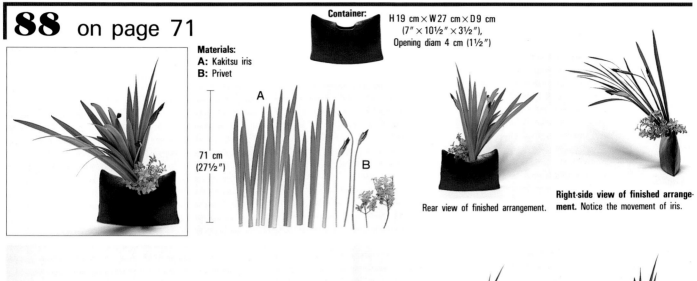

Container: H 19 cm × W 27 cm × D 9 cm
(7″ × 10½″ × 3½″),
Opening diam 4 cm (1½″)

Materials:
A: Kakitsu iris
B: Privet

71 cm
(27½″)

A

B

Rear view of finished arrangement.

Right-side view of finished arrangement. Notice the movement of iris.

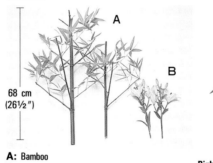

1 Set iris leaves at center left, slanting low forward.

2 Insert iris flowers in center, facing towards right.

3 Set more leaves in center pointing right.

4 Place privet at the base slanting low to finish.

92 on page 74

Container:
H 31 cm,
Opening diam 5 cm
(12″, 2″)

Materials:

A

B

68 cm
(26½″)

A: Bamboo
B: Lily
C: Colored string (red, yellow, white, navy, black)
30 wire

Right-side view of finished arrangement.

Rear view of finished arrangement. Five-colored strings fall in curvy and straight lines.

How to increase water intake of bamboo: Pierce through all the joints except the bottom, using an iron stick. Pour in hot salty water and plug up the top with wet tissue.

1 Stand bamboo in center of vase.

2 Add another stalk, inclining right.

3 Insert lilies at base to protrude forward.

4 Using # 30 wire, secure ends of navy strings at tip of bamboo. Loop the other end upwards and hang onto a higher fork.

5 Hang strings of each color separately, fixing to branches.

105

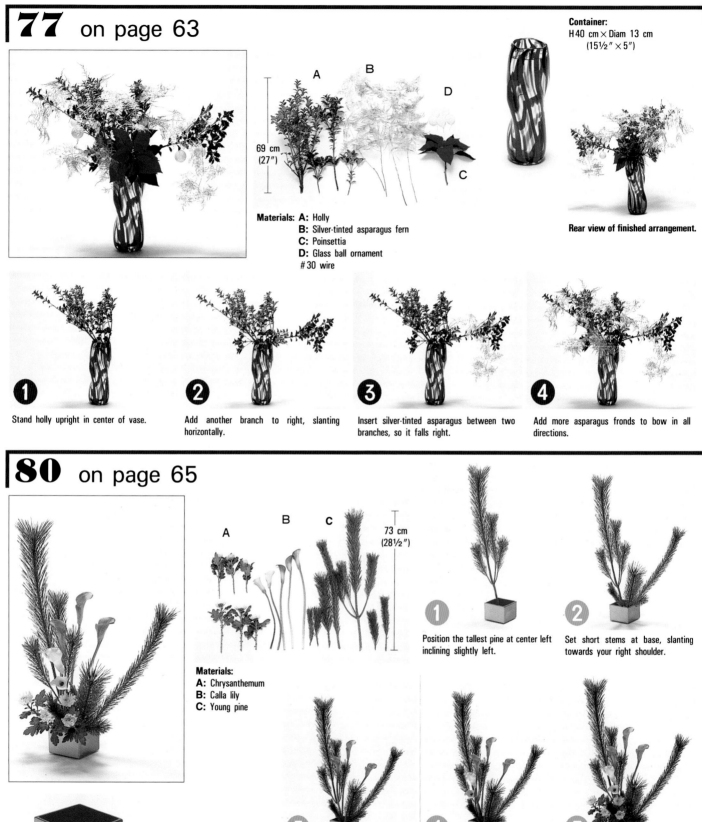

Container:
H 40 cm × Diam 13 cm
(15½″ × 5″)

69 cm
(27″)

A

B

D

C

Materials: A: Holly
B: Silver-tinted asparagus fern
C: Poinsettia
D: Glass ball ornament
#30 wire

Rear view of finished arrangement.

1 Stand holly upright in center of vase.

2 Add another branch to right, slanting horizontally.

3 Insert silver-tinted asparagus between two branches, so it falls right.

4 Add more asparagus fronds to bow in all directions.

80 on page 65

A

B

C

73 cm
(28½″)

Materials:
A: Chrysanthemum
B: Calla lily
C: Young pine

Container:
H 9 cm × W 13 cm × D 13 cm
(3½″ × 5″ × 5″)
Lay *kenzan* (needlepoint holder).

1 Position the tallest pine at center left inclining slightly left.

2 Set short stems at base, slanting towards your right shoulder.

3 Center orange calla lilies, facing forward.

4 Place yellow calla lilies on the left in varying lengths.

5 Set yellow and white chrysanthemums slanting low to conceal rim of vase.

Right-side view of finished arrangement. Notice the whole arrangement inclines forward.

Left-side view of finished arrangement.

5 Using wire, secure glass balls onto holly.

6 Finish with poinsettia, slanting forward from the base.

◀ **Right-side view of finished arrangement.** Notice the clear vertical line of young pine.

Rear view of finished arrangement. Note the clear vertical line of young pine.

◀ **Left-side view of finished arrangement.**

78 on page 63

on page 63

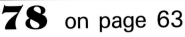

A
B
C
D
E

31 cm (12″)

Materials:
A: Dried apple slice
B: Smilax china
C: Red vine
D: Filicoides aurea (variegated cedar)
E: Eucalyptus
Ribbon
#30 wire

1 Form red vine into a ring. Lay tips of Filicoides aurea in same direction, securing with wire.

2 Continue until the ring is entirely covered with leaves.

3 Make a bow with sheer ribbon and attach to the top with wire.

4 Insert eucalyptus in the same direction all around.

5 Add smilax china all around.

6 Using wire, secure dried apple slices in good proportion.

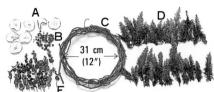

84 on page 68

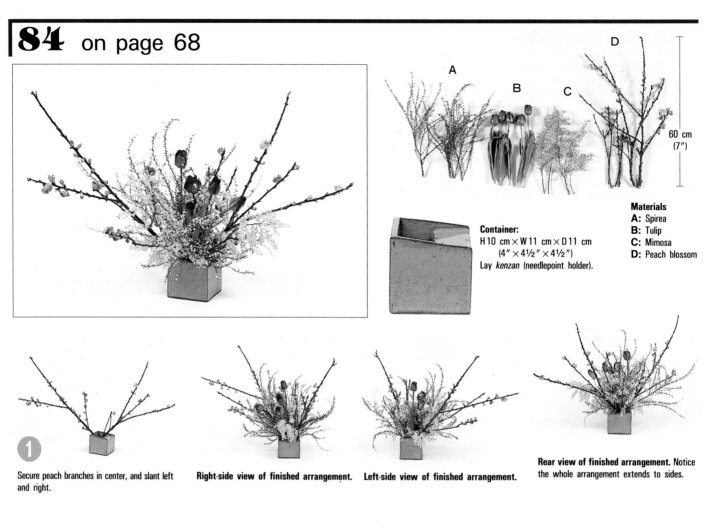

Materials
A: Spirea
B: Tulip
C: Mimosa
D: Peach blossom

60 cm (7″)

Container:
H 10 cm × W 11 cm × D 11 cm
(4″ × 4½″ × 4½″)
Lay *kenzan* (needlepoint holder).

① Secure peach branches in center, and slant left and right.

Right-side view of finished arrangement.

Left-side view of finished arrangement.

Rear view of finished arrangement. Notice the whole arrangement extends to sides.

② Add twigs of peach to back and front.

③ Place tulips in center inclining slightly right so they protrude forward.

④ Fill with mimosa framing all around tulips.

⑤ Insert short branches of spirea slanting forward, long branches behind.

81 on page 65

Materials:
A: Pine cone
B: Pine
C: Crane-shaped *mizuhiki* ornament
D: Ear of rice
E: Straw rope (40 cm / 15½″ in length)
F: *Mizuhiki* (paper cord) #30 wire

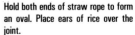

◀ **Rear view of finished arrangement.** Loop for hanging loop is attached at back.

F: Mizuhiki (paper cord) #30 wire

① Hold both ends of straw rope to form an oval. Place ears of rice over the joint.

② Bind with #30 wire as shown.

86 on page 69

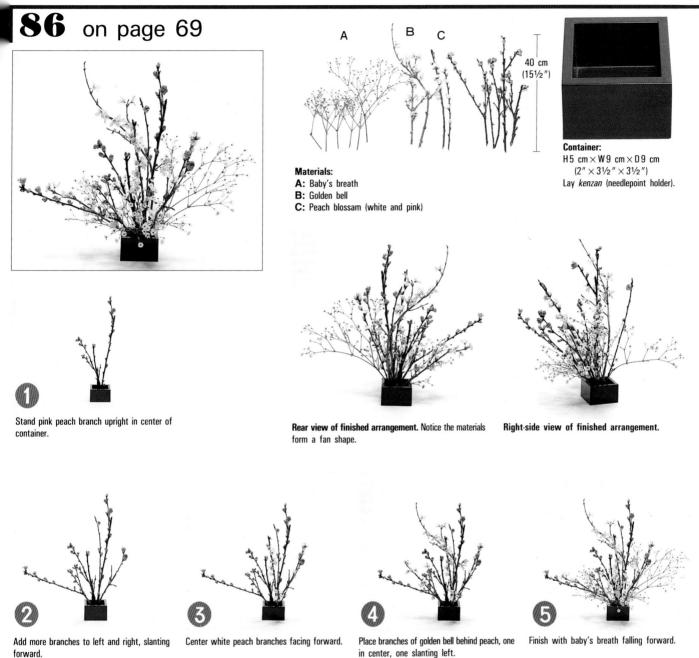

Materials:
A: Baby's breath
B: Golden bell
C: Peach blossam (white and pink)

Container:
H 5 cm × W 9 cm × D 9 cm
(2″ × 3½″ × 3½″)
Lay *kenzan* (needlepoint holder).

① Stand pink peach branch upright in center of container.

Rear view of finished arrangement. Notice the materials form a fan shape.

Right-side view of finished arrangement.

② Add more branches to left and right, slanting forward.

③ Center white peach branches facing forward.

④ Place branches of golden bell behind peach, one in center, one slanting left.

⑤ Finish with baby's breath falling forward.

③ Bind again neatly with *mizuhiki*. Secure with wire so the ends point upward.

④ Insert pine twigs, one in front of rice and one underneath.

⑤ Attach pine cone at the end ot *mizuhiki* using wire.

⑥ Insert legs of crane into pine needles so it faces left at an angle.

⑦ Attach a hanging loop of wire at back.

Rear view of finished arrangement. Note the form of variegated pine.

Right-side view of finished arrangement. Notice the vertical line of bamboo.

Container:

H 9 cm × W 35 cm × D 22 cm
(3½″ × 13½″ × 8½″)
Lay *kenzan* (needlepoint holder).

Materials:
A: Chloranthus glaber
B: Oncidium orchid
C: White plum
D: Bamboo (wrap with *washi* paper)
E: Variegated pine
F: Bamboo stalk
G: *Washi* paper (purple and gold)
Paper glue

E 72 cm (28″)

①② Layer 2 sheets of *washi*, sliding apart at one corner. Wrap bamboo with layered paper.

Secure ends with paper glue.

③ Set *kenzan* at front right of container. Stand several supporting stalks upright.

④ Place the hollow end of bamboo onto supporting stalks.

⑤ Push bamboo into *kenzan* to stand upright.

⑥ Place variegated pine behind bamboo, slanting right.

⑦ Place more pine in front, slanting forward.

⑧ Place branches of plum in center inclining to show the best shape.

⑨ Add Chloranthus glaber slanting towards your right shoulder.

⑩ Finish with oncidium by placing at center, facing front left.

82 on page 66

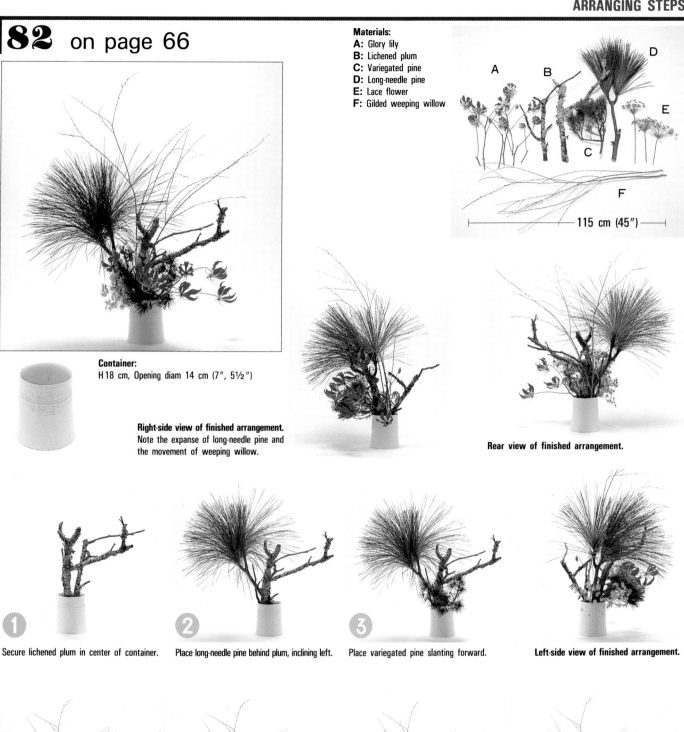

Materials:
A: Glory lily
B: Lichened plum
C: Variegated pine
D: Long-needle pine
E: Lace flower
F: Gilded weeping willow

├─ 115 cm (45″) ─┤

Container:
H 18 cm, Opening diam 14 cm (7″, 5½″)

Right-side view of finished arrangement.
Note the expanse of long-needle pine and the movement of weeping willow.

Rear view of finished arrangement.

① Secure lichened plum in center of container.

② Place long-needle pine behind plum, inclining left.

③ Place variegated pine slanting forward.

Left-side view of finished arrangement.

④ Place willow behind to cascade forward.

⑤ Place glory lily slanting almost holizontally towards front right.

⑥ Insert lily in front, slanting low.

⑦ Finish by adding lace flower low on left.

87 on page 70

Container: H 9 cm × W 31 cm × D 27 cm
(3½″ × 12″ × 10½″)
Line with *kenzan* and *kansui-seki*.

Kansui-seki: Marble-white pebbles used either to show the water surface attractive, or to give height to *kenzan* (needlepoint holder). Available at garden shops.

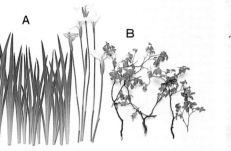

Materials: A: Sweetflag
B: Billberry

Rear view of finished arrangement. Note the whole arrangement stand almost vertically.

1 Position *kenzan* in center of container. Line the bottom with *kansui-seki*.

2 Stand the longest stem of sweetflag upright.

3 Add more stems to left, slightly inclining forward.

Right-side view of finished arrangement.

Left-side view of finished arrangement.

4 Add another sweetflag slightly inclining right.

5 Set leaves of sweetflag behind and in front of flowers.

6 Leaves are set to stand as if naturally grown.

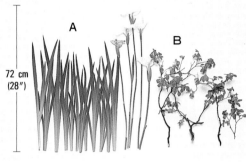

7 Add billberry behind the arrangement. Slant another branch low left.

8 Add more billberry to conceal the base.

93 on page 75

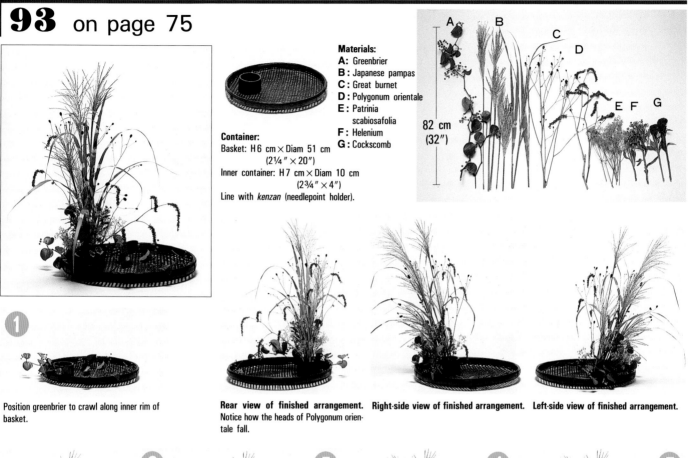

Materials:
A : Greenbrier
B : Japanese pampas
C : Great burnet
D : Polygonum orientale
E : Patrinia scabiosafolia
F : Helenium
G : Cockscomb

82 cm (32")

Container:
Basket: H 6 cm × Diam 51 cm
(2¼" × 20")
Inner container: H 7 cm × Diam 10 cm
(2¾" × 4")
Line with *kenzan* (needlepoint holder).

1

Position greenbrier to crawl along inner rim of basket.

Rear view of finished arrangement. Notice how the heads of Polygonum orientale fall.

Right-side view of finished arrangement.

Left-side view of finished arrangement.

2

Stand a tall pampas upright in center of *kenzan*.

3

Place leaves of pampas in the front to cascade naturally.

4

Add more pampas to left, inclining front left.

5

Place Helenium in the front slanting forward.

6

Place Patrinia low in front to give a light and fluffy effect.

7

Place cockscomb to the other side of helenium, slanting left.

8

Place Polygonum to hang naturally to left and right.

9

Finally add great burnet dispersing lightly over the arrangement.

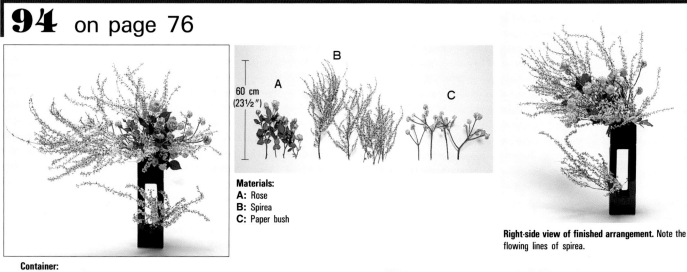

Materials:
A: Rose
B: Spirea
C: Paper bush

Right-side view of finished arrangement. Note the flowing lines of spirea.

Container:

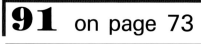

H 34 cm × W 10 cm × D 10 cm (13″ × 4″ × 4″)

Place spirea in upper opening, slanting front left.

Stand another stem upright in center.

Add another stem slanting low forward.

Place paper bush inclining low forward.

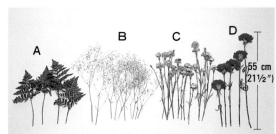

Materials: A: Leather fern   **C:** Spray carnation
B: Baby's breath   **D:** Carnation (red)

55 cm (21½″)

Right-side view of finished arrangement. Notice the directions of carnations.

Container:
H 31 cm,
Opening diam 10 cm (12″, 4″)

Put carnation resting its stem against rim of vase at a slant.

Add more carnations and pink spray carnations in same direction.

Place leather fern slanting front left. Place more carnations slanting left.

Insert a long stem of spray carnations slanting low right.

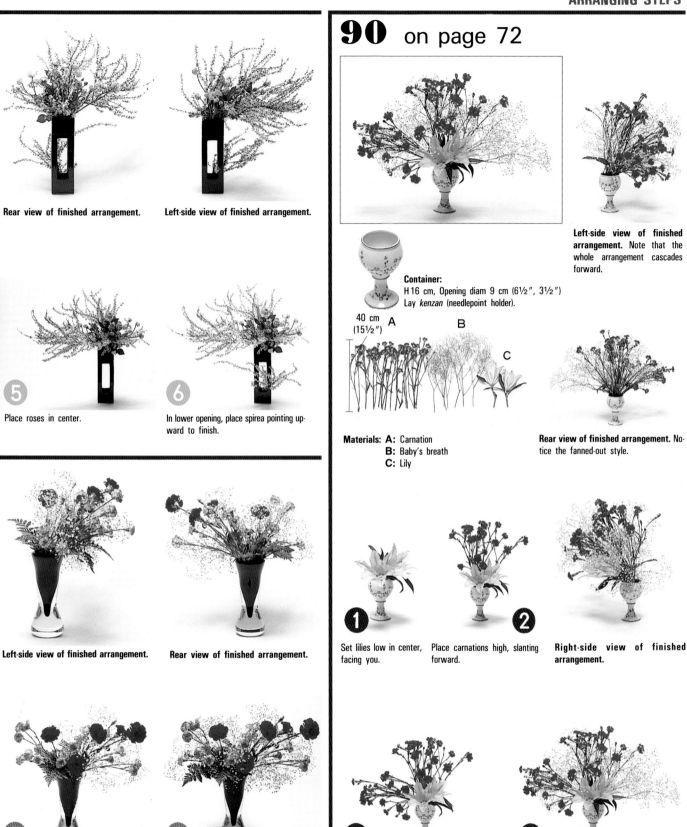

Rear view of finished arrangement.

Left-side view of finished arrangement.

⑤ Place roses in center.

⑥ In lower opening, place spirea pointing upward to finish.

Left-side view of finished arrangement.

Rear view of finished arrangement.

⑤ Insert baby's breath to disperse over carnations on the right.

⑥ Add more baby's breath to give a light and fluffy effect.

90 on page 72

Left-side view of finished arrangement. Note that the whole arrangement cascades forward.

Container:
H 16 cm, Opening diam 9 cm (6½″, 3½″)
Lay *kenzan* (needlepoint holder).

40 cm (15½″)   A   B   C

Materials: **A:** Carnation
B: Baby's breath
C: Lily

Rear view of finished arrangement. Notice the fanned-out style.

❶ Set lilies low in center, facing you.

❷ Place carnations high, slanting forward.

Right-side view of finished arrangement.

❸ Add more carnations cascading towards left.

❹ Place baby's breath behind, dispersing over the whole arrangement.

95 on page 71

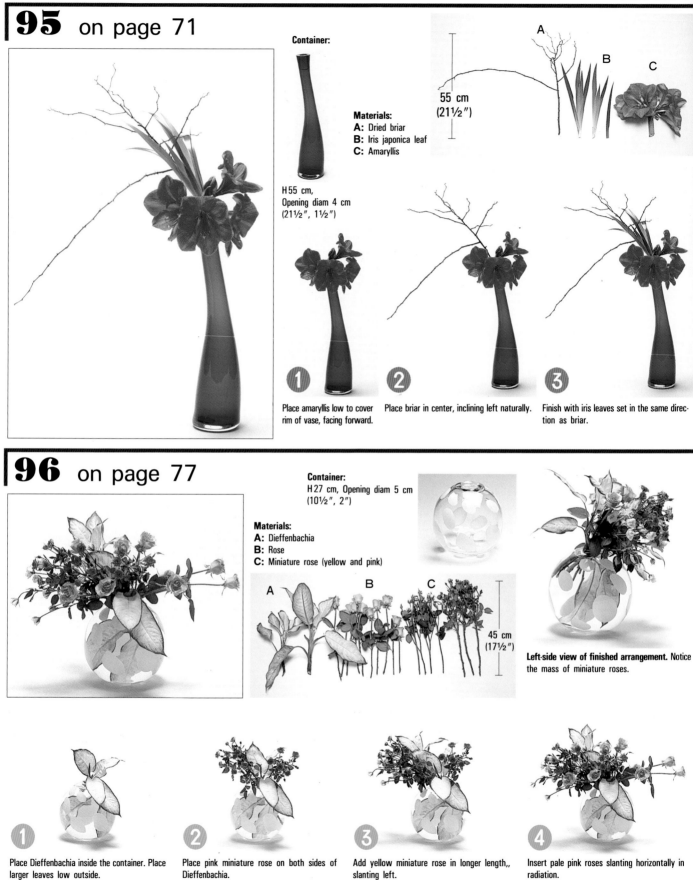

Container:

Materials:
A: Dried briar
B: Iris japonica leaf
C: Amaryllis

55 cm
(21½")

H 55 cm,
Opening diam 4 cm
(21½", 1½")

**① ** Place amaryllis low to cover rim of vase, facing forward.

**② ** Place briar in center, inclining left naturally.

**③ ** Finish with iris leaves set in the same direction as briar.

96 on page 77

Container:
H 27 cm, Opening diam 5 cm
(10½", 2")

Materials:
A: Dieffenbachia
B: Rose
C: Miniature rose (yellow and pink)

45 cm
(17½")

Left-side view of finished arrangement. Notice the mass of miniature roses.

**① ** Place Dieffenbachia inside the container. Place larger leaves low outside.

**② ** Place pink miniature rose on both sides of Dieffenbachia.

**③ ** Add yellow miniature rose in longer length,, slanting left.

**④ ** Insert pale pink roses slanting horizontally in radiation.

CHOOSING PLANT MATERIALS

Although there are no rules or taboos when choosing floral materials, it seems that some combinations are more harmonious than others. For beginners, a combination of branches and flowers is highly recommended. The strength of branches affects and complements the fragile beauty of flowers and creates a surprising effect which could not be achieved easily if either of them were used alone. In fact, there are some arranging styles using a single kind of foliage or flower, but a considerable amount of practice is essential to bend the materials. Therefore it is not appropriate for the beginners.

CUTTING METHODS

Cut away any leaves and branches that are damaged, broken, or too dense to define the stem lines clearly. If necessary, straighten a curved stem or bend a straight stem before cutting to the required length.

●Cutting a flower stem

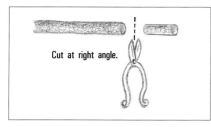

Cut at right angle.

Cut flowers quickly at right angle. Thin stems can be cut between the points of scissors whereas thicker stems can be easily cut if placed well inside the blades of the scissors. When cutting a hollow stalk such as calla lily, catch the stalk between the blades of the scissors, and rotate the stalk as you cut. Always remember that too much pressure on blades will crush the tissue of the stem.

●Cutting a branch

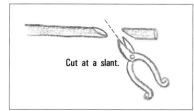

Cut at a slant.

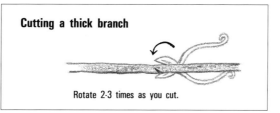

Cutting a thick branch

Rotate 2-3 times as you cut.

Cut branches diagonally so that the edges can be easily inserted into *kenzan* or pushed against the inner wall of the vase. Open the scissor handles wide, put the branch well inside the blades at an angle, and cut.

When the branch is too thick to cut with a single motion of the scissors, catch it well inside the blades and cut as far as you can. Remove scissors and repeat the same motion until completely cut. Another way of cutting a thick branch is rotating it as you cut the outside, then breaking it with both hands. A saw can be also used to cut very thick branches.

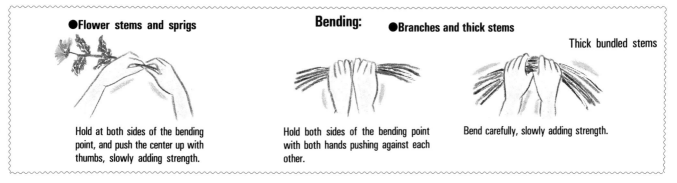

Bending:

●Flower stems and sprigs

Hold at both sides of the bending point, and push the center up with thumbs, slowly adding strength.

●Branches and thick stems

Hold both sides of the bending point with both hands pushing against each other.

Thick bundled stems

Bend carefully, slowly adding strength.

CONDITIONING METHODS

Flowers tend to wilt prematurely if cut and exposed to the air. There are several traditional devices to help the stem ends absorb water easily. Before giving any special treatment, it is essential to cut the stems deep under water.

1. Cutting under Water

This is the basic preservation method to increase water intake. Cut the stems deep under water and the pressure allows the water to be drawn up easily. Every flower must be cut this way before being treated in any of the following methods.

Good for:
All except lotus and other water plants

2. Hot Water Treatment

Some flowers such as peony or amaranth tend to wither easily. Dip cut ends of flowers into hot water 1–2 minutes and then into cold water immediately. The difference of temperatures hastens water absorption. Baby's breath lasts longer with this treatment in winter.

Good for:
Globe amaranth, Patrinia scabiosafollia, Lady's mantle, Hollyhock, Amaranth, Great burnet, Baby's breath, Peony, Scotch broom, cockscomb

3. Charring

Wrap the blossoms and leaves in wet newspaper and char the cut ends over fire. Burn until the ends glow red for 1–2 minutes, then dip into cold water immediately.

Good for:
Rose, Miniature rose, Spray mum, Croton, Poinsettia, Peach blossom

4. Crushing

Hard, fibrous stems can be conditioned in this method. Using a side of closed scissors, crush the ends about 5 cm (2″). Thinner stems such as clematis can be crushed between your teeth. Leave the stems in water before arranging. If using *kenzan*: cut some of the crushed end.

Good for:
Spirea
Balloonflower

5. Breaking

Hard and fibrous flowers such as chrysanthemum can be just broken under water. This enlarges the surface area of the stem end and speeds water intake.

Good for:
Chrysanthemum
Spray mum

6. Splitting

Holding the branch with your hand diagonal cut end up, make a cross cut quickly. This method also enlarges the surface area of the stem end and speeds water intake.

Good for:
Japanese maholia
Camellia
Flowering quince
Maple

Chemical Treatments

Wipe dry the cut edges of material before applying the chemicals. This way the chemicals will be absorbed quickly.

7. Mint oil

This is used to disinfect the cut edges. Dip the end into mint oil before arranging in the container. The stem end of clematis should be crushed with a hammer or scissors before dipping.

Good for:
Caladium, Mountain laurel, Blazing-star, Clematis, Hosta

8. Vinegar

Vinegar is used for its sterlizing effect on plants. Cut the stem end and immediately dip into vinegar before arranging.

Good for:
Bamboo, Japanese pampas, Shepherd's purse, Foxtail, Bamboo grass, Begonia, Aster, Polygonum orientale

9. Alcohol

Sake or whiskey is added to the water in the container after arranging.

Good for:
Smokegrass, Wisteria, Blazing-star

10. *Yaki-myoban* (White alum)

If the stem is spongy, white alum is used to stimulate the cut surface to allow water to be absorbed easily. Rub white alum into the cut end.

Good for:
Hydrangea, Hydrangea macrophylla normalis, Cineraria

11. Salt

Salt is especially effective for flowers in bloom from summer to autumn. The stem end should be crushed before being rubbed with salt.

Good for:
Balloonflower, Sunflower, Great burnet, Caladium, Bird's nest fern, Bamboo

12. Plant food

Flowers which have a short life span, such as a few days, will last a week by adding plant food, sold at florists.

Good for:
All flowers and foliage

FIXING TECHNIQUES

Securing method differs greatly depending on the arranging styles and the types of containers.

Fixing onto *kenzan*

●Thin stems

Push the stem end into the spikes. Push until the cut end rests on the bottom of *kenzan*. Slant the stem, if necessary, after this securing procedure. If slanting low, push the end onto the spikes with enough strength to secure the side of the stem. The following are the techniques of fixing according to the pliability and thickness of the stems:

Capping

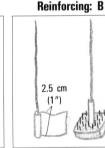

1 If the stem is sturdy but too thin to be secured in *kenzan*, it is often reinforced by capping with a thicker stem.

2 Cut 2 cm-3 cm (¾″-1⅛″) long piece from a thicker stem, and insert the thin stem into this supporting cap.

Binding	**Reinforcing: A**	**Reinforcing: B**	**Folding stems**	**Supporting**
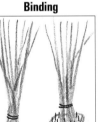		2.5 cm (1″)		A B 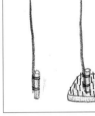
Very thin stems can be bound together using wire to add thickness.	Stems with heavy heads or fragile stems are bound together with a short branch using wire.	Very thin stems can be wrapped with paper to add thickness.	If the stem is too thin to be secured in *kenzan*, bend the end to form a "V".	

A: When slanting fragile stems, push a small piece of branch horizontally into *kenzan*, then place the stem against it.

B: Stand a small piece of branch on *kenzan*, and rest the stem on it.

●Branches

Try to push branches into the spaces between the spikes rather than into the spikes themselves. (Cut the stem so the edge is slightly wider than the interval between the spikes.)

When slanting the stem, cut the edge at a slant so the balk remains on the slanting side. Push the stem upright into *kenzan*, and carefully slant it toward the longer side. Be sure the side of remaining balm is secured on *kenzan*.

Arranging without *kenzan*

●Cross-bar fixture (fixed in vase):

From a strong and flexible branch, cut two pieces slightly longer than the diameter of the vase.

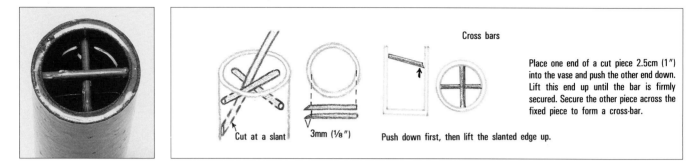

Cross bars

Place one end of a cut piece 2.5cm (1″) into the vase and push the other end down. Lift this end up until the bar is firmly secured. Secure the other piece across the fixed piece to form a cross-bar.

Cut at a slant   3mm (⅛″)

Push down first, then lift the slanted edge up.

●Vertical bar fixture (fixed on material):

When the branch has a heavy head and does not stay at a desired angle, a slit stalk is used to support it in place. Cut a piece of branch slightly shorter than the diameter of the vase. Split the end deep enough to hold the materials at the desired height. Split the end of the material and interlock with the supporting stalk in the vase. This way the material is secured at three points: the rim of the vase (**a**), the interlocking point (**b**), and the inside wall of the vase (**c**). (If the material is too thin to split, thrust it into the slit.)

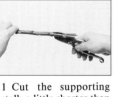

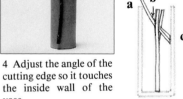

1 Cut the supporting stalk a little shorter than the height of the vase. Slit the end to the determined length.

2 Split the end slightly deeper than the interlocking point.

3 Interlock the slit material and the supporting stalk.

4 Adjust the angle of the cutting edge so it touches the inside wall of the vase.

●Direct fixing

The branch rests only on two points of the vase: the rim and the inside wall of the vase.

Techniques for direct fixing

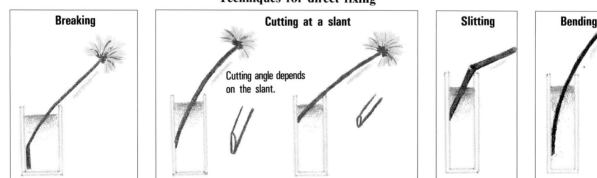

Breaking

Cutting at a slant
Cutting angle depends on the slant.

Slitting

Bending

IKEBANA CONTAINERS

Ikebana is never complete without an appropriate container. Consider the shape, color, size and texture of the container to match the floral materials.

Suiban (shallow container)

There are various shapes such as round, oval, rectangular, or triangular. One that has a 30 cm (11¾″) diameter and a 4 cm–5 cm (1½″–2″) height is most recommended.

Tall Vase

The most practical vase would be about 30 cm–40 cm (11¾″–15½″) high, and 10 cm–15 cm (4″–5¾″) wide cylinder or prism type.

Compote

Compote shaped container is used specially for a modern arrangement or when a certain height is required.

Pot

Choose a heavy, stable pot with a small opening. When arranging, turn the pot around and check the best side to match the floral materials.

Bowl

Look around your house and find a possible container to match the arrangement.

Glass containers

Clarity and freshness of glass create a mood not only for summer but for any season and any style: traditional or modern. Exposing the water is another feature of this kind of container, but special attention should be paid to the immersed stems.

Basket or Colander

Bamboo-woven baskets and colanders go well with floral materials because both are made of plants. Arrangements in woven containers create a warm and natural impression. Natural bamboo colander complements wild flowers picked in the field or in your garden. Be sure the water container is stable in the basket.

121

IKEBANA UTENSILS

Scissors:

There are a few kinds of scissors or shears specially made for ikebana. Choose whichever is easy for you to handle. When cutting a branch, place the cutting point between the blades of scissors as deep as possible, and grasp firmly. Thicker branches can be easily cut by slitting the side of the cutting point. Rub oil on your scissors after every use to prevent from rusting.

Handling scissors:

1 Hold the upper handle between your thumb and palm, the lower handle with your fingers.

2 Hold tightly, without putting any finger between the handles.

Kenzan

Kenzan, or needlepoint holders, come in various shapes and sizes. They can hold the materials at any angle and they can be rearranged many times. Choose a heavy one with lots of spikes.

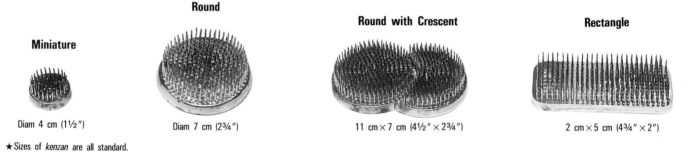

Miniature

Diam 4 cm (1½″)

Round

Diam 7 cm (2¾″)

Round with Crescent

11 cm × 7 cm (4½″ × 2¾″)

Rectangle

2 cm × 5 cm (4¾″ × 2″)

★Sizes of *kenzan* are all standard.

Kenzan repairer:

Thick branches could easily bend the *kenzan* spikes. In this case, a needle repairer is used to straighten the spikes.

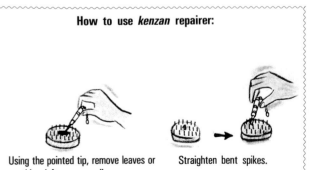

How to use *kenzan* repairer:

Using the pointed tip, remove leaves or anything left among spikes.

Straighten bent spikes.

BASICS & TECHNIQUES OF IKEBANA

Saws:

When the branches are too thick or too hard to cut with scissors, this is a great helping hand. A small folding saw made specially for ikebana is very convenient and easy to carry when you go outdoors.

Wire:

Thin wire can be used to bind materials together. There are straight and rolled lengths of wire in different thicknesses and colors. Green-colored wire is most versatile. Choose #30 wire in the matching color.

Bowl:

A deep bowl is used to cut materials under water to keep them fresh longer.

Water spray:

For a floral display placed in a dry area or in an air-conditioned room, it is essential to give extra water occasionally, because the flowers absorb water through the petals and leaves as well as up through the stem. Also, spray water over the finished arrangement. It will wash off any dirt or dust on leaves.

Kansui-seki (mable-white pebbles):

Varieties of pebbles and marbles are used to hide and to give weight to *kenzan*. Choose pebbles that match the color of flowers. Glass beads can also look nice if used in a glass container.

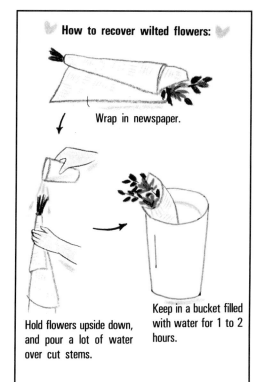

How to recover wilted flowers:

Wrap in newspaper.

Hold flowers upside down, and pour a lot of water over cut stems.

Keep in a bucket filled with water for 1 to 2 hours.

INDEX OF FLOWERS

Note: Page numbers in *italics* indicate instructions.